JUSTICE

A Tragedy in Four Acts

JOHN GALSWORTHY

With school and acting notes by
JOHN HAMPDEN, M.A.

DUCKWORTH

This impression 1977
First published February 1910
Twenty-seventh impression December 1959
This edition 1964
Reprinted June 1965, *May* 1968
Reprinted in larger format 1977

Editorial matter © 1964 by
Gerald Duckworth & Co. Ltd.

Gerald Duckworth & Co. Ltd.
The Old Piano Factory
43 Gloucester Crescent, London N.W.1

ISBN 0 7156 1221 2 (cased)
0 7156 1222 0 (paper)

*All applications respecting amateur performances of
John Galsworthy's plays must be made to*

THE SECRETARY
INCORPORATED SOCIETY OF AUTHORS
84 DRAYTON GARDENS, LONDON S.W.10

All other applications to the Author's Agents

MESSRS CURTIS BROWN LIMITED
1 CRAVEN HILL
LONDON W.2
AND 60 E. 56 ST.
NEW YORK 10022
U.S.A.

*First performed at
the Duke of York's Theatre, London,
on February* 21*st,* 1910

Printed in Great Britain by
Unwin Brothers Limited
The Gresham Press, Old Woking, Surrey

CONTENTS

CHARACTERS OF THE PLAY

JAMES HOW
WALTER HOW, *his son* } *solicitors*

ROBERT COKESON, *their managing clerk*

WILLIAM FALDER, *their junior clerk*

SWEEDLE, *their office-boy*

WISTER, *a dectective*

COWLEY, *a cashier*

MR. JUSTICE FLOYD, *judge*

HAROLD CLEAVER, *an old advocate*

HECTOR FROME, *a young advocate*

CAPTAIN DANSON, *V.C.*, *a prison governor*

THE REV. HUGH MILLER, *a prison chaplain*

EDWARD CLEMENTS, *a prison doctor*

WOODER, *a chief warder*

MOANEY
CLIPTON } *convicts*
O'CLEARY

RUTH HONEYWILL, *a woman*

A NUMBER OF BARRISTERS, SOLICITORS, SPECTATORS, USHERS, REPORTERS, JURYMEN, WARDERS AND PRISONERS

TIME: *About* 1910.   PLACE: *England*
ACT I.   *The office of James and Walter How. Morning. July.*
ACT II.   *Assizes. Afternoon. October.*
ACT III.   *A prison. December.*
    SCENE I.   *The Governor's office.*
    SCENE II.   *A corridor.*
    SCENE III.   *A cell.*
ACT IV.   *The office of James and Walter How. Morning.*
    March two years later.

ACT I

The scene is the managing clerk's room, at the offices of JAMES AND WALTER HOW, *on a July morning. The room is old-fashioned, furnished with well-worn mahogany and leather, and lined with tin boxes and estate plans. It has three doors. Two of them are close together in the centre of a wall. One of these two doors leads to the outer office, which is only divided from the managing clerk's room by a partition of wood and clear glass; and when the door into this outer office is opened there can be seen the wide outer door leading out on to the stone stairway of the building. The other of these two centre doors leads to the junior clerks' room. The third door is that leading to the partners' room.*

The managing clerk, COKESON, *is sitting at his table adding up figures in a pass-book, and murmuring their numbers to himself. He is a man of sixty, wearing spectacles; rather short, with a bald head, and an honest, pug-dog face. He is dressed in a well-worn black frock-coat and pepper-and-salt trousers.*

COKESON. And five's twelve, and three—fifteen, nineteen, twenty-three, thirty-two, forty-one—and carry four. [*He ticks the page, and goes on murmuring.*] Five, seven, twelve, seventeen, twenty-four and nine, thirty-three, thirteen and carry one.

[*He again makes a tick. The outer office door is opened, and* SWEEDLE, *the office-boy, appears, closing the door behind him. He is a pale youth of sixteen, with spiky hair.*

COKESON. [*With grumpy expectation*] And carry one.

SWEEDLE. There's a party wants to see Falder, Mr. Cokeson.

COKESON. Five, nine, sixteen, twenty-one, twenty-nine—and carry two. Sent him to Morris's. What name?

SWEEDLE. Honeywill.

3

COKESON.   What's his business?

SWEEDLE.   It's a woman.

COKESON.   A lady?

SWEEDLE.   No, a person.

COKESON.   Ask her in.   Take this pass-book to Mr. James.
                                        [*He closes the pass-book.*

SWEEDLE. [*Reopening the door*] Will you come in, please?

[RUTH HONEYWILL *comes in.   She is a tall woman, twenty-six
years old, unpretentiously dressed, with black hair and eyes, and an
ivory-white, clear-cut face.   She stands very still, having a
natural dignity of pose and gesture.*

[SWEEDLE *goes out into the partners' room with the pass-book.*

COKESON.   [*Looking round at* RUTH] The young man's out.
[*Suspiciously.*]   State your business, please.

RUTH.   [*Who speaks in a matter-of-fact voice, and with a
slight West-country accent*] It's a personal matter, sir.

COKESON.   We don't allow private callers here.   Will you
leave a message?

RUTH.   I'd rather see him, please.

        [*She narrows her dark eyes and gives him a honeyed look.*

COKESON.   [*Expanding*] It's all against the rules.   Suppose
I had *my* friends here to see me!   It'd never do!

RUTH.   No, sir.

COKESON.   [*A little taken aback*] Exactly!   And here you
are wanting to see a *junior* clerk!

RUTH.   Yes, sir; I must see him.

COKESON.   [*Turning full round to her with a sort of outraged
interest*] But this is a lawyer's office.   Go to his private address.

RUTH.   He's not there.

COKESON.   [*Uneasy*] Are you related to the party?

RUTH.   No, sir.

COKESON.   [*In real embarrassment*] I don't know what to
say.   It's no affair of the office.

RUTH.   But what am I to do?

COKESON.   Dear me! I can't tell you that.

[SWEEDLE *comes back.   He crosses to the outer office and passes through into it, with a quizzical look at* COKESON, *carefully leaving the door an inch or two open.*

COKESON. [*Fortified by this look*] This won't do, you know, this won't do at all. Suppose one of the partners came in!

[*An incoherent knocking and chuckling is heard from the outer door of the outer office.*

SWEEDLE. [*Putting his head in*] There's some children outside here.

RUTH. They're mine, please.

SWEEDLE. Shall I hold them in check?

RUTH. They're quite small, sir. [*She takes a step towards* COKESON.

COKESON. You mustn't take up his time in office hours; we're a clerk short as it is.

RUTH. It's a matter of life and death.

COKESON. [*Again outraged*] Life and death!

SWEEDLE. Here *is* Falder.

[FALDER *has entered through the outer office. He is a pale, good-looking young man, with quick, rather scared eyes. He moves towards the door of the clerks' office, and stands there irresolute.*

COKESON. Well, I'll give you a minute. It's not regular.

[*Taking up a bundle of papers, he goes out into the partners' room.*

RUTH. [*In a low, hurried voice*] He's on the drink again, Will. He tried to cut my throat last night. I came out with the children before he was awake. I went round to you——

FALDER. I've changed my digs.

RUTH. Is it all ready for to-night?

FALDER. I've got the tickets. Meet me 11.45 at the booking office. For God's sake don't forget we're man and wife! [*Looking at her with tragic intensity.*] Ruth!

RUTH. You're not afraid of going, are you?

FALDER. Have you got your things, and the children's?

RUTH. Had to leave them, for fear of waking Honeywill, all but one bag. I can't go near home again.

FALDER. [*Wincing*] All that money gone for nothing. How much *must* you have?

RUTH.   Six pounds—I could do with that, I think.

FALDER.   Don't give away where we're going. [*As if to himself*] When I get out there I mean to forget it all.

RUTH.   If you're sorry, say so.   I'd sooner he killed me than take you against your will.

FALDER.   [*With a queer smile*] We've *got* to go.   I don't care; I'll have *you*.

RUTH.   You've just to say; it's not too late.

FALDER.   It *is* too late.   Here's seven pounds.   Booking office—11.45 to-night.   If you weren't what you are to me, Ruth——!

RUTH.   Kiss me!

[*They cling together passionately, then fly apart just as* COKESON *re-enters the room.* RUTH *turns and goes out through the outer office.* COKESON *advances deliberately to his chair and seats himself.*

COKESON.   This isn't right, Falder.

FALDER.   It shan't occur again, sir.

COKESON.   It's an improper use of these premises.

FALDER.   Yes, sir.

COKESON.   You quite understand—the party was in some distress;   and, having children with her, I allowed my feelings—— [*He opens a drawer and produces from it a tract.*] Just take this!   "Purity in the Home."   It's a well-written thing.

FALDER.   [*Taking it, with a peculiar expression*] Thank you, sir.

COKESON.   And look here, Falder, before Mr. Walter comes, have you finished up that cataloguing Davis had in hand before he left?

FALDER.   I shall have done with it to-morrow, sir—for good.

COKESON.   It's over a week since Davis went.   Now it won't do, Falder.   You're neglecting your work for private life.   I shan't mention about the party having called, but——

FALDER.   [*Passing into his room*] Thank you, sir.

[COKESON *stares at the door through which* FALDER *has gone out; then shakes his head, and is just settling down to write, when* WALTER HOW *comes in through the outer office. He is a rather refined-looking man of thirty-five, with a pleasant, almost apologetic voice.*

WALTER.   Good-morning, Cokeson.

COKESON.   Morning, Mr. Walter.

WALTER.   My father here?

COKESON.   [*Always with a certain patronage as to a young man who might be doing better*] Mr. James has been here since eleven o'clock.

WALTER.   I've been in to see the pictures, at the Guildhall.

COKESON.   [*Looking at him as though this were exactly what was to be expected*] Have you now—ye-es. This lease of Boulter's—am I to send it to counsel?

WALTER.   What does my father say?

COKESON.   'Aven't bothered him.

WALTER.   Well, we can't be too careful.

COKESON.   It's such a little thing—hardly worth the fees. I thought you'd do it yourself.

WALTER.   Send it, please. I don't want the responsibility.

COKESON.   [*With an indescribable air of compassion*] Just as you like. This "right-of-way" case—we've got 'em on the deeds.

WALTER.   I know; but the intention was obviously to exclude that bit of common ground.

COKESON.   We needn't worry about that. We're the *right* side of the law.

WALTER.   I don't like it.

COKESON.   [*With an indulgent smile*] We shan't want to set ourselves up against the law. Your father wouldn't waste his time doing that.

[*As he speaks* JAMES HOW *comes in from the partners' room. He is a shortish man, with white side-whiskers, plentiful grey hair, shrewd eyes, and gold pince-nez.*]

JAMES.   Morning, Walter.

WALTER.   How are you, father?

COKESON. [*Looking down his nose at the papers in his hand as though deprecating their size*] I'll just take Boulter's lease in to young Falder to draft the instructions.

[*He goes out into* FALDER'S *room.*

WALTER.   About that right-of-way case?

JAMES.   Oh, well, we must go forward there.   I thought you told me yesterday the firm's balance was over four hundred.

WALTER.   So it is.

JAMES.   [*Holding out the pass-book to his son*] Three—five—one, no recent cheques.   Just get me out the cheque-book.

[WALTER *goes to a cupboard, unlocks a drawer, and produces a cheque-book.*

JAMES.   Tick the pounds in the counterfoils.   Five, fifty-four, seven, five, twenty-eight, twenty, ninety, eleven, fifty-two, seventy-one.   Tally?

WALTER.   [*Nodding*] Can't understand.   Made sure it was over four hundred.

JAMES.   Give me the cheque-book.   [*He takes the cheque-book and cons the counterfoils.*]   What's this ninety?

WALTER.   Who drew it?

JAMES.   You.

WALTER.   [*Taking the cheque-book*] July 7th?   That's the day I went down to look over the Trenton Estate—last Friday week; I came back on the Tuesday, you remember.   But look here, father, it was *nine* I drew a cheque for.   Five guineas to Smithers and my expenses.   It just covered all but half a crown.

JAMES.   [*Gravely*] Let's look at that ninety cheque.   [*He sorts the cheque out from the bundle in the pocket of the pass-book.*]   Seems all right.   There's no nine here.   This is bad.   Who cashed that nine-pound cheque?

WALTER.   [*Puzzled and pained*] Let's see!   I was finishing Mrs. Reddy's will—only just had time; yes—I gave it to Cokeson.

JAMES.   Look at that *ty*: that yours?

WALTER.   [*After consideration*] My *y's* curl back a little; this doesn't.

JAMES. [*As* COKESON *re-enters from* FALDER'S *room*] We must ask him. Just come here and carry your mind back a bit, Cokeson. D'you remember cashing a cheque for Mr. Walter last Friday week—the day he went to Trenton?

COKESON. Ye-es. Nine pounds.

JAMES. Look at this. [*Handing him the cheque.*

COKESON. No! Nine pounds. My lunch was just coming in; and of course I *like* it hot; I gave the cheque to Davis to run round to the bank. He brought it back, all notes—you remember, Mr. Walter, you wanted some silver to pay your cab. [*With a certain contemptuous compassion.*] Here, let *me* see. You've got the wrong cheque.

[*He takes cheque-book and pass-book from* WALTER.

WALTER. Afraid not.

COKESON. [*Having seen for himself*] It's funny.

JAMES. You gave it to Davis, and Davis sailed for Australia on Monday. Looks black, Cokeson.

COKESON. [*Puzzled and upset*] Why this'd be a felony! No, no! there's some mistake.

JAMES. I hope so.

COKESON. There's never been anything of that sort in the office the twenty-nine years I've been here.

JAMES. [*Looking at cheque and counterfoil*] This is a very clever bit of work; a warning to you not to leave space after your figures, Walter.

WALTER. [*Vexed*] Yes, I know—I was in such a tearing hurry that afternoon.

COKESON. [*Suddenly*] This has upset me.

JAMES. The counterfoil altered too—very deliberate piece of swindling. What was Davis's ship?

WALTER. *City of Rangoon.*

JAMES. We ought to wire and have him arrested at Naples; he can't be there yet.

COKESON. His poor young wife. I liked the young man. Dear, oh dear! In this office!

WALTER. Shall I go to the bank and ask the cashier?

JAMES. [*Grimly*] Bring him round here. And ring up Scotland Yard.

WALTER. Really?

[*He goes out through the outer office. JAMES paces the room. He stops and looks at COKESON, who is disconsolately rubbing the knees of his trousers.*

JAMES. Well, Cokeson! There's something in character, isn't there?

COKESON. [*Looking at him over his spectacles*] I don't quite take you, sir.

JAMES. Your story would sound d——d thin to anyone who didn't know you.

COKESON. Ye-es! [*He laughs. Then with sudden gravity*] I'm sorry for that young man. I feel it as if it was my own son, Mr. James.

JAMES. A nasty business!

COKESON. It unsettles you. All goes on regular, and then a thing like this happens. Shan't relish my lunch to-day.

JAMES. As bad as that, Cokeson?

COKESON. It makes you think. [*Confidentially*] He must have had temptation.

JAMES. Not so fast. We haven't convicted him yet.

COKESON. I'd sooner have lost a month's salary than had this happen. [*He broods.*

JAMES. I hope that fellow will hurry up.

COKESON. [*Keeping things pleasant for the cashier*] It isn't fifty yards, Mr. James. He won't be a minute.

JAMES. The idea of dishonesty about this office—it hits me hard, Cokeson. [*He goes towards the door of the partners' room.*

SWEEDLE. [*Entering quietly, to COKESON in a low voice*] She's popped up again, sir—something she forgot to say to Falder.

COKESON. [*Roused from his abstraction*] Eh? Impossible. Send her away!

JAMES. What's that?

COKESON. Nothing, Mr. James. A private matter. Here, I'll come myself. [*He goes into the outer office as JAMES passes *into the partners' room.*]   Now, you really mustn't—we can't have anybody just now.

RUTH.   Not for a minute, sir?

COKESON.   Reely! Reely! I can't have it.   If you want him, wait about; he'll be going out for his lunch directly.

RUTH.   Yes, sir.

[WALTER, *entering with the cashier, passes* RUTH *as she leaves the outer office.*

COKESON.   [*To the cashier, who resembles a sedentary dragoon*] Good-morning.   [*To* WALTER] Your father's in there.

[WALTER *crosses and goes into the partners' room.*

COKESON.   It's a nahsty, unpleasant little matter, Mr. Cowley.   I'm quite ashamed to have to trouble you.

COWLEY.   I remember the cheque quite well.   [*As if it were a liver.*]   Seemed in perfect order.

COKESON.   Sit down, won't you?   I'm not a sensitive man, but a thing like this about the place—it's not nice.   I like people to be open and jolly together.

COWLEY.   Quite so.

COKESON.   [*Button-holing him, and glancing towards the partners' room*] Of course he's a young man.   I've told him about it before now—leaving space after his figures, but he *will* do it.

COWLEY.   I should remember the person's face—quite a youth.

COKESON.   I don't think we shall be able to show him to you, as a matter of fact.

[JAMES *and* WALTER *have come back from the partners' room.*

JAMES.   Good-morning, Mr. Cowley.   You've seen my son and myself, you've seen Mr. Cokeson, and you've seen Sweedle, my office-boy.   It was none of us, I take it.

[*The cashier shakes his head with a smile.*

JAMES.   Be so good as to sit here.   Cokeson, engage Mr. Cowley in conversation, will you?

[*He goes towards* FALDER'S *room.*

COKESON.   Just a word, Mr. James.

JAMES.   Well?

COKESON.   You don't want to upset the young man in there, do you? He's a nervous young feller.

JAMES.   This must be thoroughly cleared up, Cokeson, for the sake of Falder's name, to say nothing of yours.

COKESON.   [*With some dignity*] That'll look after itself, sir. He's been upset once this morning; I don't want him startled again.

JAMES.   It's a matter of form; but I can't stand upon niceness over a thing like this—too serious. Just talk to Mr. Cowley.

[*He opens the door of* FALDER'S *room.*

JAMES.   Bring in the papers in Boulter's lease, will you, Falder?

COKESON.   [*Bursting into voice*] Do you keep dogs?

[*The cashier, with his eyes fixed on the door, does not answer.*

COKESON.   You haven't such a thing as a bulldog pup you could spare me, I suppose?

[*At the look on the cashier's face his jaw drops, and he turns to see* FALDER *standing in the doorway, with his eyes fixed on* COWLEY, *like the eyes of a rabbit fastened on a snake.*

FALDER.   [*Advancing with the papers*] Here they are, sir.

JAMES.   [*Taking them*] Thank you.

FALDER.   Do you want me, sir?

JAMES.   No, thanks!

[FALDER *turns and goes back into his own room. As he shuts the door* JAMES *gives the cashier an interrogative look, and the cashier nods.*

JAMES.   Sure?   This isn't as we suspected.

COWLEY.   Quite.   He knew me.   I suppose he can't slip out of that room?

COKESON.   [*Gloomily*] There's only the window—a whole floor and a basement.

[*The door of* FALDER'S *room is quietly opened, and* FALDER, *with his hat in his hand, moves towards the door of the outer office.*

JAMES.   [*Quietly*] Where are you going, Falder?

FALDER.   To have my lunch, sir.

JAMES. Wait a few minutes, would you? I want to speak to you about this lease.

FALDER. Yes, sir. [*He goes back into his room.*

COWLEY. If I'm wanted, I can swear that's the young man who cashed the cheque. It was the last cheque I handled that morning before my lunch. These are the numbers of the notes he had. [*He puts a slip of paper on the table; then, brushing his hat round*] Good-morning!

JAMES. Good-morning, Mr. Cowley!

COWLEY. [*To* COKESON] Good-morning.

COKESON. [*With stupefaction*] Good-morning.

[*The cashier goes out through the outer office.* COKESON *sits down in his chair, as though it were the only place left in the morass of his feelings.*

WALTER. What are you going to do?

JAMES. Have him in. Give me the cheque and the counterfoil.

COKESON. I don't understand. I thought young Davis——

JAMES. We shall see.

WALTER. One moment, father: have you thought it out?

JAMES. Call him in!

COKESON. [*Rising with difficulty and opening* FALDER's *door; hoarsely*] Step in here a minute. [FALDER *comes in.*

FALDER. [*Impassively*] Yes, sir?

JAMES. [*Turning to him suddenly with the cheque held out*] You know this cheque, Falder?

FALDER. No, sir.

JAMES. Look at it. You cashed it last Friday week.

FALDER. Oh! yes, sir; that one—Davis gave it me.

JAMES. I know. And you gave Davis the cash?

FALDER. Yes, sir.

JAMES. When Davis gave you the cheque was it exactly like this?

FALDER. Yes, I think so, sir.

JAMES. You know that Mr. Walter drew that cheque for *nine* pounds?

FALDER. No, sir—ninety.

JAMES. Nine, Falder.

FALDER. [*Faintly*] I don't understand, sir.

JAMES. The suggestion, of course, is that the cheque was altered; whether by you or Davis is the question.

FALDER. I—I——

COKESON. Take your time, take your time.

FALDER. [*Regaining his impassivity*] Not by me, sir.

JAMES. The cheque was handed to Cokeson by Mr. Walter at one o'clock; we know that because Mr. Cokeson's lunch had just arrived.

COKESON. I couldn't leave it.

JAMES. Exactly; he therefore gave the cheque to Davis. It was cashed by you at 1.15. We know that because the cashier recollects it for the last cheque he handled before *his* lunch.

FALDER. Yes, sir, Davis gave it to me because some friends were giving him a farewell luncheon.

JAMES. [*Puzzled*] You accuse Davis, then?

FALDER. I don't know, sir—it's very funny.

[WALTER, *who has come close to his father, says something to him in a low voice.*

JAMES. Davis was not here again after that Saturday, was he?

COKESON. [*Anxious to be of assistance to the young man, and seeing faint signs of their all being jolly once more*] No, he sailed on the Monday.

JAMES. Was he, Falder?

FALDER. [*Very faintly*] No, sir.

JAMES. Very well, then, how do you account for the fact that this nought was added to the nine in the counterfoil on or after *Tuesday*?

COKESON. [*Surprised*] How's that?

[FALDER *gives a sort of lurch; he tries to pull himself together, but he has gone all to pieces.*

JAMES. [*Very grimly*] Out, I'm afraid, Cokeson. The cheque-book remained in Mr. Walter's pocket till he came back from Trenton on Tuesday morning. In the face of this, Falder, do you still deny that you altered both cheque and counterfoil?

FALDER. No, sir—no, Mr. How. I did it, sir; I did it.

COKESON. [*Succumbing to his feelings*] Dear, dear! what a thing to do!

FALDER. I wanted the money so badly, sir. I didn't know what I was doing.

COKESON. However such a thing could have come into your head!

FALDER. [*Grasping at the words*] I can't think, sir, really! It was just a minute of madness.

JAMES. A long minute, Falder. [*Tapping the counterfoil.*] Four days at least.

FALDER. Sir, I swear I didn't know what I'd done till afterwards, and then I hadn't the pluck. Oh! sir, look over it! I'll pay the money back—I will, I promise.

JAMES. Go into your room.

[FALDER, *with a swift imploring look, goes back into his room. There is silence.*

JAMES. About as bad a case as there could be.

COKESON. To break the law like that—in here!

WALTER. What's to be done?

JAMES. Nothing for it. Prosecute.

WALTER. It's his first offence.

JAMES. [*Shaking his head*] I've grave doubts of that. Too neat a piece of swindling altogether.

COKESON. I shouldn't be surprised if he was tempted.

JAMES. Life's one long temptation, Cokeson.

COKESON. Ye-es, but I'm speaking of the flesh and the devil, Mr. James. There was a woman come to see him this morning.

WALTER. The woman we passed as we came in just now. Is it his wife?

COKESON. No, no relation. [*Restraining what in jollier circumstances would have been a wink.*] A married person, though.

WALTER. How do you know?

COKESON. Brought her children. [*Scandalized.*] There they were outside the office.

JAMES. A real bad egg.

WALTER.   I should like to give him a chance.

JAMES.   I can't forgive him for the sneaky way he went to work—counting on our suspecting young Davis if the matter came to light.   It was the merest accident the cheque-book stayed in your pocket.

WALTER.   It *must* have been the temptation of a moment. He hadn't time.

JAMES.   A man doesn't succumb like that in a moment, if he's a clean mind and habits.   He's rotten; got the eyes of a man who can't keep his hands off when there's money about.

WALTER.   [*Dryly*] We hadn't noticed that before.

JAMES.   [*Brushing the remark aside*] I've seen lots of those fellows in my time.   No doing anything with them except to keep 'em out of harm's way.   They've got a blind spot.

WALTER.   It's penal servitude.

COKESON.   They're *nahsty* places—prisons.

JAMES.   [*Hesitating*] I don't see how it's possible to spare him. Out of the question to keep him in this office—honesty's the *sine qua non.*

COKESON.   [*Hypnotized*] Of course it *is.*

JAMES.   Equally out of the question to send him out amongst people who've no knowledge of his character.   One must think of society.

WALTER.   But to brand him like this?

JAMES.   If it had been a straightforward case I'd give him another chance.   It's far from that.   He has dissolute habits.

COKESON.   I didn't say that—extenuating circumstances.

JAMES.   Same thing.   He's gone to work in the most cold-blooded way to defraud his employers, and cast the blame on an innocent man.   If that's not a case for the law to take its course, I don't know what is.

WALTER.   For the sake of his future, though.

JAMES.   [*Sarcastically*] According to you, no one would ever prosecute.

WALTER.   [*Nettled*] I hate the idea of it.

COKESON.   We must have protection.

JAMES.   This is degenerating into talk.

> [*He moves towards the partners' room.*

WALTER.   Put yourself in his place, father.

JAMES.   You ask too much of me.

WALTER.   We can't possibly tell the pressure there was on him.

JAMES.   You may depend on it, my boy, if a man is going to do this sort of thing he'll do it, pressure or no pressure; if he isn't nothing'll make him.

WALTER.   He'll never do it again.

COKESON.   [*Fatuously*] S'pose I were to have a talk with him. We don't want to be hard on the young man.

JAMES.   That'll do, Cokeson.   I've made up my mind.

> [*He passes into the partners' room.*

COKESON.   [*After a doubtful moment*] We must excuse your father.   I don't want to go against your father; if he thinks it right.

WALTER.   Confound it, Cokeson! why don't you back me up?   You know you feel——

COKESON.   [*On his dignity*] I really can't say what I feel.

WALTER.   We shall regret it.

COKESON.   He must have known what he was doing.

WALTER.   [*Bitterly*] "The quality of mercy is not strained."

COKESON.   [*Looking at him askance*] Come, come, Mr. Walter.   We must try and see it sensible.

SWEEDLE.   [*Entering with a tray*] Your lunch, sir.

COKESON.   Put it down!

[*While* SWEEDLE *is putting it down on* COKESON'S *table, the detective,* WISTER, *enters the outer office, and, finding no one there, comes to the inner doorway.   He is a square, medium-sized man, clean-shaved, in a serviceable blue serge suit and strong boots.*

WISTER. [*To* WALTER] From Scotland Yard, sir.   Detective-Sergeant Wister.

WALTER.   [*Askance*] Very well!   I'll speak to my father.

> [*He goes in to the partners' room.   JAMES enters.*

JAMES.   Morning!

> [*In answer to an appealing gesture from* COKESON.]

I'm sorry; I'd stop short of this if I felt I could.   Open that door.   [SWEEDLE, *wondering and scared, opens it.*]   Come here, Mr. Falder.

[*As* FALDER *comes shrinkingly out, the detective, in obedience to a sign from* JAMES, *slips his hand out and grasps his arm.*

FALDER.   [*Recoiling*] Oh! no—oh! no!

WISTER.   Come, come, there's a good lad.

JAMES.   I charge him with felony.

FALDER.   Oh, sir!   There's someone—I did it for her. Let me be till to-morrow.

[JAMES *motions with his head.   At that sign of hardness,* FALDER *becomes rigid.   Then, turning, he goes out quietly in the detective's grip.* JAMES *follows, stiff and erect.* SWEEDLE, *rushing to the door with open mouth, pursues them through the outer office into the corridor.   When they have all disappeared* COKESON *spins completely round and makes a rush for the outer office.*

COKESON.   [*Hoarsely*] Here!   Here!   What are we doing?

[*There is silence.   He takes out his handkerchief and mops the sweat from his face.   Going back blindly to his table, he sits down, and stares blankly at his lunch.*

The curtain falls.

ACT II

A Court of Justice, on a foggy October afternoon—crowded with barristers, solicitors, reporters, ushers, and jurymen. Sitting in the large, solid dock is FALDER, *with a warder on either side of him, placed there for his safe custody, but seemingly indifferent to and unconscious of his presence.* FALDER *is sitting exactly opposite to the* JUDGE, *who, raised above the clamour of the court, also seems unconscious of and indifferent to everything.* HAROLD CLEAVER, *the counsel for the Crown, is a dried, yellowish man, of more than middle age, in a wig worn almost to the colour of his face.* HECTOR FROME, *the counsel for the defence, is a young, tall man, clean-shaved, in a very white wig. Among the spectators, having already given their evidence, are* JAMES *and* WALTER HOW, *and* COWLEY, *the cashier.* WISTER, *the detective, is just leaving the witness-box.*

CLEAVER.   That is the case for the Crown, me lud!

                [Gathering his robes together, he sits down.

FROME.   [*Rising and bowing to the* JUDGE] If it please your lordship and members of the jury.   I am not going to dispute the fact that the prisoner altered this cheque, but I am going to put before you evidence as to the condition of his mind, and to submit that you would not be justified in finding that he was responsible for his actions at the time.   I am going to show you, in fact, that he did this in a moment of aberration, amounting to temporary insanity, caused by the violent distress under which he was labouring.   Gentlemen, the prisoner is only twenty-three years old.   I shall call before you a woman from whom you will learn the events that led up to this act.   You will hear from her own lips the tragic circumstances of her life, the still more tragic infatuation with which she has inspired the prisoner. This woman, gentlemen, has been leading a miserable existence

19

with a husband who habitually ill-uses her, from whom she actually goes in terror of her life.   I am not, of course, saying that it's either right or desirable for a young man to fall in love with a married woman, or that it's his business to rescue her from an ogre-like husband.   I'm not saying anything of the sort.   But we all know the power of the passion of love; and I would ask you to remember, gentlemen, in listening to her evidence, that, married to a drunken and violent husband, she has no power to get rid of him; for, as you know, another offence besides violence is necessary to enable a woman to obtain a divorce; and of this offence it does not appear that her husband is guilty.

JUDGE.   Is this relevant, Mr. Frome?

FROME.   My lord, I submit, extremely—I shall be able to show your lordship that directly.

JUDGE.   Very well.

FROME.   In these circumstances, what alternatives were left to her?   She could either go on living with this drunkard, in terror of her life; or she could apply to the Court for a separation order.   Well, gentlemen, my experience of such cases assures me that this would have given her very insufficient protection from the violence of such a man; and even if effectual would very likely have reduced her either to the workhouse or the streets—for it's not easy, as she is now finding, for an unskilled woman without means of livelihood to support herself and her children without resorting either to the Poor Law or—to speak quite plainly—to the sale of her body.

JUDGE.   You are ranging rather far, Mr. Frome.

FROME.   I shall fire point-blank in a minute, my lord.

JUDGE.   Let us hope so.

FROME.   Now, gentlemen, mark—and this is what I have been leading up to—this woman will tell you, and the prisoner will confirm her, that, confronted with such alternatives, she set her whole hopes on himself, knowing the feeling with which she had inspired him.   She saw a way out of her misery by going with him to a new country, where they would both be unknown, and might pass as husband and wife. This was a desperate and, as my friend Mr. Cleaver will no doubt call it, an immoral resolution; but, as a fact, the minds of both of them were constantly turned towards it. One wrong is no excuse for another, and those who are never likely to be faced by such a situation possibly have the right to hold up their hands—as to that I prefer to say nothing. But whatever view you take, gentlemen, of this part of the prisoner's story—whatever opinion you form of the right of these two young people under such circumstances to take the law into their own hands—the fact remains that this young woman in her distress, and this young man, little more than a boy, who was so devotedly attached to her, *did* conceive this—if you like—reprehensible design of going away together. Now, for that, of course, they required money, and—they had none. As to the actual events of the morning of July 7th, on which this cheque was altered, the events on which I rely to prove the defendant's irresponsibility —I shall allow those events to speak for themselves, through the lips of my witnesses. Robert Cokeson. [*He turns, looks round, takes up a sheet of paper, and waits.*]

[COKESON *is summoned into court, and goes into the witness-box, holding his hat before him. The oath is administered to him.*

FROME. What is your name?

COKESON. Robert Cokeson.

FROME. Are you managing clerk to the firm of solicitors who employ the prisoner?

COKESON. Ye-es.

FROME. How long had the prisoner been in their employ?

COKESON. Two years. No, I'm wrong there—all but seventeen days.

FROME. Had you him under your eye all that time?

COKESON. Except Sundays and holidays.

FROME. Quite so. Let us hear, please, what you have to say about his general character during those two years.

COKESON. [*Confidentially to the jury, and as if a little surprised at being asked*] He was a nice, pleasant-spoken young

man.   I'd no fault to find with him—quite the contrary.   It
was a *great* surprise to me when he did a thing like that.

FROME.   Did he ever give you reason to suspect his honesty?

COKESON.   No!   To have dishonesty in our office, that'd
never do.

FROME.   I'm sure the jury fully appreciate that, Mr. Cokeson.

COKESON.   Every man of business knows that honesty's the
sign qua nonne.

FROME.   Do you give him a good character all round, or do
you not?

COKESON.   [*Turning to the* JUDGE] Certainly.   We were all
very jolly and pleasant together, until this happened.   Quite
upset me.

FROME.   Now, coming to the morning of the 7th of July,
the morning on which the cheque was altered.   What have you
to say about his demeanour that morning?

COKESON.   [*To the jury*] If you ask me, I don't think he was
quite compos when he did it.

THE JUDGE.   [*Sharply*] Are you suggesting that he was insane?

COKESON.   Not compos.

THE JUDGE.   A little more precision, please.

FROME.   [*Smoothly*] Just tell us, Mr. Cokeson.

COKESON.   [*Somewhat outraged*] Well, in my opinion—
[*looking at the* JUDGE]—such as it is—he was jumpy at the time.
The jury will understand my meaning.

FROME.   Will you tell us how you came to that conclusion?

COKESON.   Ye-es, I will.   I have my lunch in from the
restaurant, a chop and a potato—saves time.   That day it
happened to come just as Mr. Walter How handed me the
cheque.   Well, I like it hot; so I went into the clerks' office
and I handed the cheque to Davis, the other clerk, and told him
to get change.   I noticed young Falder walking up and down.
I said to him: "This is not the Zoological Gardens, Falder."

FROME.   Do you remember what he answered?

COKESON.   Ye-es: "I wish to God it were!"   Struck me as
funny.

FROME.   Did you notice anything else peculiar?

COKESON.   I did.

FROME.   What was that?

COKESON.   His collar was unbuttoned.   Now, I like a young man to be neat.   I said to him: "Your collar's unbuttoned."

FROME.   And what did he answer?

COKESON.   Stared at me.   It wasn't nice.

THE JUDGE.   Stared at you?   Isn't that a very common practice?

COKESON.   Ye-es, but it was the look in his eyes.   I can't explain my meaning—it was funny.

FROME.   Had you ever seen such a look in his eyes before?

COKESON.   No.   If I had I should have spoken to the partners. We can't have anything eccentric in our profession.

THE JUDGE.   Did you speak to them on that occasion?

COKESON.   [*Confidentially*] Well, I didn't like to trouble them without prime facey evidence.

FROME.   But it made a very distinct impression on your mind?

COKESON. Ye-es. The clerk Davis could have told you the same.

FROME.   Quite so.   It's very unfortunate that we've not got him here.   Now can you tell me of the morning on which the discovery of the forgery was made?   That would be the 18th.   Did anything happen that morning?

COKESON.   [*With his hand to his ear*] I'm a little deaf.

FROME.   Was there anything in the course of that morning— I mean before the discovery—that caught your attention?

COKESON.   Ye-es—a woman.

THE JUDGE.   How is *this* relevant, Mr. Frome?

FROME.   I am trying to establish the state of mind in which the prisoner committed this act, my lord.

THE JUDGE.   I quite appreciate that.   But this was long after the act.

FROME.   Yes, my lord, but it contributes to my contention.

THE JUDGE.   Well!

FROME.   You say a woman.   Do you mean that she came to the office?

COKESON.   Ye-es.

FROME.   What for?

COKESON.   Asked to see young Falder; he was out at the moment.

FROME.   Did you see her?

COKESON.   I did.

FROME.   Did she come alone?

COKESON.   [*Confidentially*] Well, there you put me in a difficulty.   I mustn't tell you what the office-boy told me.

FROME.   Quite so, Mr. Cokeson, quite so——

COKESON.   [*Breaking in with an air of "You are young— leave it to me"*] But I think we can get round it.   In answer to a question put to her by a third party the woman said to me: "They're mine, sir."

THE JUDGE.   What are?   What were?

COKESON.   Her children.   They were outside.

THE JUDGE.   How do you know?

COKESON.   Your lordship musn't ask me that, or I shall have to tell you what I was told—and that'd never do.

THE JUDGE.   [*Smiling*] The office-boy made a statement.

COKESON.   Egg-zactly.

FROME.   What I want to ask you, Mr. Cokeson, is this.   In the course of her appeal to see Falder, did the woman say anything that you specially remember?

COKESON.   [*Looking at him as if to encourage him to complete the sentence*] A leetle more, sir.

FROME.   Or did she not?

COKESON.   She did.   I shouldn't like you to have led me to the answer.

FROME.   [*With an irritated smile*] Will you tell the jury what it was?

COKESON.   "It's a matter of life and death."

FOREMAN OF THE JURY.   Do you mean the woman said that?

COKESON.   [*Nodding*] It's not the sort of thing you like to have said to you.

FROME.   [*A little impatiently*] Did Falder come in while she was there? [COKESON *nods*.] And she saw him, and went away?

COKESON. Ah! there I can't follow you. I didn't see her go.

FROME. Well, is she there now?

COKESON. [*With an indulgent smile*] No!

FROME. Thank you, Mr. Cokeson.   [*He sits down.*

CLEAVER. [*Rising*] You say that on the morning of the forgery the prisoner was jumpy. Well, now, sir, what precisely do you mean by that word?

COKESON. [*Indulgently*] I *want* you to understand. Have you ever seen a dog that's lost its master? He was kind of everywhere at once with his eyes.

CLEAVER. Thank you; I was coming to his eyes. You called them "funny." What are we to understand by that. Strange, or what?

COKESON. Ye-es, funny.

CLEAVER. [*Sharply*] Yes, sir, but what may be funny to you may not be funny to me, or to the jury. Did they look frightened, or shy, or fierce, or what?

COKESON. You make it very hard for me. I give you the word, and you want me to give you another.

CLEAVER. [*Rapping his desk*] Does "funny" mean mad?

COKESON. Not mad, fun——

CLEAVER. Very well! Now you say he had his collar unbuttoned? Was it a hot day?

COKESON. Ye-es; I think it was.

CLEAVER. And did he button it when you called his attention to it?

COKESON. Ye-es, I think he did.

CLEAVER. Would you say that that denoted insanity?

[*He sits down.* COKESON, *who has opened his mouth to reply, is left gaping.*

FROME. [*Rising hastily*] Have you ever caught him in that dishevelled state before?

COKESON. No! He was *always* clean and quiet.

FROME. That will do, thank you.

[COKESON *turns blandly to the* JUDGE, *as though to rebuke counsel for not remembering that the* JUDGE *might wish to have a chance; arriving at the conclusion that he is to be asked nothing further, he turns and descends from the box, and sits down next to* JAMES *and* WALTER.

FROME.   Ruth Honeywill.

[RUTH *comes into court, and takes her stand stoically in the witness-box.   She is sworn.*

FROME.   What is your name, please?

RUTH.   Ruth Honeywill.

FROME.   How old are you?

RUTH.   Twenty-six.

FROME.   You are a married woman, living with your husband?   A little louder.

RUTH.   No, sir; not since July.

FROME.   Have you any children?

RUTH.   Yes, sir, two.

FROME.   Are they living with you?

RUTH.   Yes, sir.

FROME.   You know the prisoner?

RUTH.   [*Looking at him*] Yes.

FROME.   What was the nature of your relations with him?

RUTH.   We were friends.

THE JUDGE.   Friends?

RUTH.   [*Simply*] Lovers, sir.

THE JUDGE.   [*Sharply*] In what sense do you use that word?

RUTH.   We love each other.

THE JUDGE.   Yes, but——

RUTH.   [*Shaking her head*] No, your lordship—not yet.

THE JUDGE.   Not yet!   H'm! [*He looks from* RUTH *to* FALDER.]   Well!

FROME.   What is your husband?

RUTH.   Traveller.

FROME.   And what was the nature of your married life?

RUTH.   [*Shaking her head*] It don't bear talking about.

FROME.   Did he ill-treat you, or what?

RUTH. Ever since my first was born.

FROME. In what way?

RUTH. I'd rather not say. All sorts of ways.

THE JUDGE. I am afraid I must stop this, you know.

RUTH. [*Pointing to* FALDER] *He* offered to take me out of it, sir. We were going to South America.

FROME. [*Hastily*] Yes, quite—and what prevented you?

RUTH. I was outside his office when he was taken away. It nearly broke my heart.

FROME. You knew, then, that he had been arrested?

RUTH. Yes, sir. I called at his office afterwards, and [*pointing to* COKESON] that gentleman told me all about it.

FROME. Now, do you remember the morning of Friday, July 7th?

RUTH. Yes.

FROME. Why?

RUTH. My husband nearly strangled me that morning.

THE JUDGE. Nearly strangled you!

RUTH. [*Bowing her head*] Yes, my lord.

FROME. With his hands, or——?

RUTH. Yes, I just managed to get away from him. I went straight to my friend. It was eight o'clock.

THE JUDGE. In the morning? Your husband was not under the influence of liquor then?

RUTH. It wasn't always that.

FROME. In what condition were you?

RUTH. In very bad condition, sir. My dress was torn, and I was half choking.

FROME. Did you tell your friend what had happened?

RUTH. Yes. I wish I never had.

FROME. It upset him?

RUTH. Dreadfully.

FROME. Did he ever speak to you about a cheque?

RUTH. Never.

FROME. Did he ever give you any money?

RUTH. Yes.

FROME.   When was that?

RUTH.   On Saturday.

FROME.   The 8th?

RUTH.   To buy an outfit for me and the children, and get all ready to start.

FROME.   Did that surprise you, or not?

RUTH.   What, sir?

FROME.   That he had money to give you.

RUTH.   Yes, because on the morning when my husband nearly killed me my friend cried because he hadn't the money to get me away.   He told me afterwards he'd come into a windfall.

FROME.   And when did you last see him?

RUTH.   The day he was taken away, sir.   It was the day we were to have started.

FROME.   Oh, yes, the morning of the arrest.   Well, did you see him at all between the Friday and that morning?   [RUTH *nods.*]   What was his manner then?

RUTH.   Dumb-like—sometimes he didn't seem able to say a word.

FROME.   As if something unusual had happened to him?

RUTH.   Yes.

FROME.   Painful, or pleasant, or what?

RUTH.   Like a fate hanging over him.

FROME.   [*Hesitating*] Tell me, did you love the defendant very much?

RUTH.   [*Bowing her head*] Yes.

FROME.   And had he a very great affection for you?

RUTH.   [*Looking at* FALDER] Yes, sir.

FROME.   Now, ma'am, do you or do you not think that your danger and unhappiness would seriously affect his balance, his control over his actions?

RUTH.   Yes.

FROME.   His reason, even?

RUTH.   For a moment like, I think it would.

FROME.   Was he very much upset that Friday morning, or was he fairly calm?

RUTH.   Dreadfully upset.   I could hardly bear to let him go from me.

FROME.   Do you still love him?

RUTH.   [*With her eyes on* FALDER] He's ruined himself for me.

FROME.   Thank you.

[*He sits down.*   RUTH *remains stoically upright in the witness-box.*

CLEAVER.   [*In a considerate voice*] When you left him on the morning of Friday the 7th you would not say that he was out of his mind, I suppose?

RUTH.   No, sir.

CLEAVER.   Thank you; I've no further questions to ask you.

RUTH.   [*Bending a little forward to the jury*] I would have done the same for him; I would indeed.

THE JUDGE.   Please, please!   You say your married life is an unhappy one?   Faults on both sides?

RUTH.   Only that I never bowed down to him.   I don't see why I should, sir, not to a man like that.

THE JUDGE.   You refused to obey him?

RUTH.   [*Avoiding the question*] I've always studied him to keep things nice.

THE JUDGE.   Until you met the prisoner—was that it?

RUTH.   No; even after that.

THE JUDGE.   I ask, you know, because you seem to me to glory in this affection of yours for the prisoner.

RUTH.   [*Hesitating*] I—I do.   It's the only thing in my life now.

THE JUDGE.   [*Staring at her hard*] Well, step down, please.

[RUTH *looks at* FALDER, *then passes quietly down and takes her seat among the witnesses.*

FROME.   I call the prisoner, my lord.

[FALDER *leaves the dock; goes into the witness-box, and is duly sworn.*

FROME.   What is your name?

FALDER.   William Falder.

FROME.   And age?

FALDER.   Twenty-three.

FROME.   You are not married?   [FALDER *shakes his head.*

FROME.   How long have you known the last witness?

FALDER.   Six months.

FROME.   Is her account of the relationship between you a correct one?

FALDER.   Yes.

FROME.   You became devotedly attached to her, however?

FALDER.   Yes.

THE JUDGE.   Though you knew she was a married woman?

FALDER.   I couldn't help it, your lordship.

THE JUDGE.   Couldn't help it?

FALDER.   I didn't seem able to.

[*The* JUDGE *slightly shrugs his shoulders.*

FROME.   How did you come to know her?

FALDER.   Through my married sister.

FROME.   Did you know whether she was happy with her husband?

FALDER.   It was trouble all the time.

FROME.   You knew her husband?

FALDER.   Only through her—he's a brute.

THE JUDGE.   I can't allow indiscriminate abuse of a person not present.

FROME.   [*Bowing*] If your lordship pleases.   [*To* FALDER.] You admit altering this cheque?   [FALDER *bows his head.*

FROME.   Carry your mind, please, to the morning of Friday, July the 7th, and tell the jury what happened.

FALDER.   [*Turning to the jury*] I was having my breakfast when she came.   Her dress was all torn, and she was gasping and couldn't seem to get her breath at all; there were the marks of his fingers round her throat; her arm was bruised, and the blood had got into her eyes dreadfully.   It frightened me, and then when she told me, I felt—I felt—well—it was too much for me!   [*Hardening suddenly.*]   If you'd seen it, having the feelings for her that I had, you'd have felt the same, I know.

FROME.   Yes?

FALDER. When she left me—because I had to go to the office—I was out of my senses for fear that he'd do it again, and thinking what I could do. I couldn't work—all the morning I was like that—simply couldn't fix my mind on anything. I couldn't think at all. I seemed to have to keep moving. When Davis—the other clerk—gave me the cheque—he said· "It'll do you good, Will, to have a run with this. You seem half off your chump this morning." Then when I had it in my hand —I don't know how it came, but it just flashed across me that if I put the *ty* and the nought there would be the money to get her away. It just came and went—I never thought of it again. Then Davis went out to his luncheon, and I don't really remember what I did till I'd pushed the cheque through to the cashier under the rail. I remember his saying "Notes?" Then I suppose I knew what I'd done. Anyway, when I got outside I wanted to chuck myself under a bus; I wanted to throw the money away; but it seemed I was in for it, so I thought at any rate I'd save her. Of course the tickets I took for the passage and the little I gave her's been wasted, and all, except what I was obliged to spend myself, I've restored. I keep thinking over and over however it was I came to do it, and how I can't have it all again to do differently!

[FALDER *is silent, twisting his hands before him.*

FROME. How far is it from your office to the bank?

FALDER. Not more than fifty yards, sir.

FROME. From the time Davis went out to lunch to the time you cashed the cheque, how long do you say it must have been?

FALDER. It couldn't have been four minutes, sir, because I ran all the way.

FROME. During those four minutes you say you remember nothing?

FALDER. No, sir; only that I ran.

FROME. Not even adding the *ty* and the nought?

FALDER. No, sir. I don't really.

[FROME *sits down, and* CLEAVER *rises.*

CLEAVER. But you remember running, do you?

FALDER.   I was all out of breath when I got to the bank.

CLEAVER.   And you don't remember altering the cheque?

FALDER.   [*Faintly*] No, sir.

CLEAVER.   Divested of the romantic glamour which my friend is casting over the case, is this anything but an ordinary forgery?   Come.

FALDER.   I was half frantic all that morning, sir.

CLEAVER.   Now, now!   You don't deny that the *ty* and the nought were so like the rest of the handwriting as to thoroughly deceive the cashier?

FALDER.   It was an accident.

CLEAVER.   [*Cheerfully*] Queer sort of accident, wasn't it? On which day did you alter the counterfoil?

FALDER.   [*Hanging his head*] On the Wednesday morning.

CLEAVER.   Was that an accident too?

FALDER.   [*Faintly*] No.

CLEAVER.   To do that you had to watch your opportunity, I suppose?

FALDER.   [*Almost inaudibly*] Yes.

CLEAVER.   You don't suggest that you were suffering under great excitement when you did that?

FALDER.   I was haunted.

CLEAVER.   With the fear of being found out?

FALDER.   [*Very low*] Yes.

THE JUDGE.   Didn't it occur to you that the only thing for you to do was to confess to your employers, and restore the money?

FALDER.   I was afraid.   [*There is silence.*

CLEAVER.   You desired, too, no doubt, to complete your design of taking this woman away?

FALDER.   When I found I'd done a thing like that, to do it for nothing seemed so dreadful.   I might just as well have chucked myself into the river.

CLEAVER.   You knew that the clerk Davis was about to leave England—didn't it occur to you when you altered this cheque that suspicion would fall on him?

FALDER. It was all done in a moment. I thought of it afterwards.

CLEAVER. And that didn't lead you to avow what you'd done?

FALDER. [*Sullenly*] I meant to write when I got out there—I would have repaid the money.

THE JUDGE. But in the meantime your innocent fellow-clerk might have been prosecuted.

FALDER. I knew he was a long way off, your lordship. I thought there'd be time. I didn't think they'd find it out so soon.

FROME. I might remind your lordship that as Mr. Walter How had the cheque-book in his pocket till after Davis had sailed, if the discovery had been made only one day later Falder himself would have left, and suspicion would have attached to him, and not to Davis, from the beginning.

THE JUDGE. The question is whether the prisoner knew that suspicion would light on himself, and not on Davis. [*To* FALDER *sharply*.] Did you know that Mr. Walter How had the cheque-book till after Davis had sailed?

FALDER. I—I—thought—he——

THE JUDGE. Now speak the truth—yes or no!

FALDER. [*Very low*] No, my lord. I had no means of knowing.

THE JUDGE. That disposes of your point, Mr. Frome.

[FROME *bows to the* JUDGE.

CLEAVER. Has any aberration of this nature ever attacked you before?

FALDER. [*Faintly*] No, sir.

CLEAVER. You had recovered sufficiently to go back to your work that afternoon?

FALDER. Yes, I had to take the money back.

CLEAVER. You mean the *nine* pounds. Your wits were sufficiently keen for you to remember that? And you still persist in saying you don't remember altering this cheque.

[*He sits down.*

FALDER. If I hadn't been mad I should never have had the courage.

FROME.   [*Rising*] Did you have your lunch before going
back?

FALDER.   I never ate a thing all day; and at night I couldn't
sleep.

FROME.   Now, as to the four minutes that elapsed between
Davis's going out and your cashing the cheque: do you say that
you recollect *nothing* during those four minutes?

FALDER.   [*After a moment*] I remember thinking of Mr.
Cokeson's face.

FROME.   Of Mr. Cokeson's face!   Had that any connection
with what you were doing?

FALDER.   No, sir.

FROME.   Was that in the office, before you ran out?

FALDER.   Yes, and while I was running.

FROME.   And that lasted till the cashier said: "Will you
have notes?"

FALDER.   Yes, and then I seemed to come to myself—and
it was too late.

FROME.   Thank you.   That closes the evidence for the
defence, my lord.

[*The* JUDGE *nods, and* FALDER *goes back to his seat in the dock.*

FROME.   [*Gathering up notes*] If it please your Lordship—
Members of the Jury,—My friend in cross-examination has
shown a disposition to sneer at the defence which has been set up
in this case, and I am free to admit that nothing I can say will
move you, if the evidence has not already convinced you that the
prisoner committed this act in a moment when to all practical
intents and purposes he was not responsible for his actions; a
moment of such mental and moral vacuity, arising from the
violent emotional agitation under which he had been suffering,
as to amount to temporary madness.   My friend has alluded to
the "romantic glamour" with which I have sought to invest
this case.   Gentlemen, I have done nothing of the kind.   I
have merely shown you the background of "life"—that palpitat-
ing life which, believe me—whatever my friend may say—
always lies behind the commission of a crime.   Now, gentlemen,

we live in a highly civilized age, and the sight of brutal violence disturbs us in a very strange way, even when we have no personal interest in the matter. But when we see it inflicted on a woman whom we love—what then? Just think of what your own feelings would have been, each of you, at the prisoner's age; and then look at him. Well! he is hardly the comfortable, shall we say bucolic, person likely to contemplate with equanimity marks of gross violence on a woman to whom he was devotedly attached. Yes, gentlemen, look at him! He has not a strong face; but neither has he a vicious face. He is just the sort of man who would easily become the prey of his emotions. You have heard the description of his eyes. My friend may laugh at the word "funny"—*I* think it better describes the peculiar uncanny look of those who are strained to breaking-point than any other word which could have been used. I don't pretend, mind you, that his mental irresponsibility was more than a flash of darkness, in which all sense of proportion became lost; but I do contend that, just as a man who destroys himself at such a moment may be, and often is, absolved from the stigma attaching to the crime of self-murder, so he may, and frequently does, commit other crimes while in this irresponsible condition, and that he may as justly be acquitted of criminal intent and treated as a patient. I admit that this is a plea which might well be abused. It is a matter for discretion. But here you have a case in which there is every reason to give the benefit of the doubt. You heard me ask the prisoner what he thought of during those four fatal minutes. What was his answer? "I thought of Mr. Cokeson's face?" Gentlemen, no man could invent an answer like that; it is absolutely stamped with truth. You have seen the great affection (legitimate or not) existing between him and this woman, who came here to give evidence for him at the risk of her life. It is impossible for you to doubt his distress on the morning when he committed this act. We well know what terrible havoc such distress can make in weak and highly nervous people. It was all the work of a moment. The rest has followed, as death follows a stab to the heart, or water drops if

you hold up a jug to empty it.   Believe me, gentlemen, there is
nothing more tragic in life than the utter impossibility of chang-
ing what you have done.   Once this cheque was altered and
presented, the work of four minutes—four mad minutes—the
rest has been silence.   But in those four minutes the boy before
you has slipped through a door, hardly opened, into that great
cage which never again quite lets a man go—the cage of the
Law.   His further acts, his failure to confess, the alteration of
the counterfoil, his preparations for flight, are all evidence—
not of deliberate and guilty intention when he committed the
prime act from which these subsequent acts arose; no—they are
merely evidence of the weak character which is clearly enough
his misfortune.   But is a man to be lost because he is bred
and born with a weak character?   Gentlemen, men like the
prisoner are destroyed daily under our law for want of that
human insight which sees them as they are, patients, and not
criminals.   If the prisoner be found guilty, and treated as
though he were a criminal type, he will, as all experience shows,
in all probability become one.   I beg you not to return a verdict
that may thrust him back into prison and brand him for ever.
Gentlemen, Justice is a machine that, when someone has once
given it the starting push, rolls on of itself.   Is this young man
to be ground to pieces under this machine for an act which at
the worst was one of weakness?   Is he to become a member of
the luckless crews that man those dark, ill-starred ships called
prisons?   Is that to be his voyage—from which so few return?
Or is he to have another chance, to be still looked on as one who
has gone a little astray, but who will come back?   I urge you,
gentlemen, do not ruin this young man!   For, as a result of
those four minutes, ruin, utter and irretrievable, stares him in
the face.   He can be saved now.   Imprison him as a criminal,
and I affirm to you that he will be lost.   He has neither the face
nor the manner of one who can survive that terrible ordeal.
Weigh in the scales his criminality and the suffering he has
undergone.   The latter is ten times heavier already.   He has
lain in prison under this charge for more than two months.   Is

he likely ever to forget that? Imagine the anguish of his mind during that time. He has had his punishment, gentlemen, you may depend. The rolling of the chariot-wheels of Justice over this boy began when it was decided to prosecute him. We are now already at the second stage. If you permit it to go on to the third I would not give—that for him.

[*He holds up finger and thumb in the form of a circle, drops his hand, and sits down.*

[*The jury stir, and consult each other's faces; then they turn towards the counsel for the Crown, who rises, and, fixing his eyes on a spot that seems to give him satisfaction, slides them every now and then towards the jury.*

CLEAVER. May it please your Lordship. [*Rising on his toes.*] Gentlemen of the Jury,—The facts in this case are not disputed, and the defence, if my friend will allow me to say so, is so thin that I don't propose to waste the time of the Court by taking you over the evidence. The plea is one of temporary insanity. Well, gentlemen, I daresay it is clearer to me than it is to you why this rather—what shall we call it?—bizarre defence has been set up. The alternative would have been to plead guilty. Now, gentlemen, if the prisoner had pleaded guilty my friend would have had to rely on a simple appeal to his lordship. Instead of that, he has gone into the byways and hedges and found this—er—peculiar plea, which has enabled him to show you the proverbial woman, to put her in the box— to give, in fact, a romantic glow to this affair. I compliment my friend; I think it highly ingenious of him. By these means, he has—to a certain extent—got round the Law. He has brought the whole story of motive and stress out in court, at first hand, in a way that he would not otherwise have been able to do. But when you have once grasped that fact, gentlemen, you have grasped everything. [*With good-humoured contempt.*] For look at this plea of insanity; we can't put it lower than that. You have heard the woman. She has every reason to favour the prisoner, but what did she say? She said that the prisoner was *not* insane when she left him in the morning. If he were

going out of his mind through distress, that was obviously the
moment when insanity would have shown itself.   You have
heard the managing clerk, another witness for the defence.
With some difficulty I elicited from him the admission that the
prisoner, though jumpy (a word that he seemed to think you
would understand, gentlemen, and I'm sure I hope you do), was
not mad when the cheque was handed to Davis.   I agree with
my friend that it's unfortunate that we have not got Davis here,
but the prisoner has told you the words with which Davis in
turn handed him the cheque; he obviously, therefore, was *not*
mad when he received it, or he would not have remembered
those words.   The cashier has told you that he was certainly in
his senses when he cashed it.   We have therefore the plea that
a man who is sane at ten minutes past one, and sane at fifteen
minutes past, may, for the purposes of avoiding the consequences
of a crime, call himself insane between those points of time.
Really, gentlemen, this is so peculiar a proposition that I am not
disposed to weary you with further argument.   You will form
your own opinion of its value.   My friend has adopted this way
of saying a great deal to you—and very eloquently—on the score
of youth, temptation, and the like.   I might point out, however,
that the offence with which the prisoner is charged is one of the
most serious known to our law; and there are certain features
in this case, such as the suspicion which he allowed to rest on his
innocent fellow-clerk, and his relations with this married woman,
which will render it difficult for you to attach too much import-
ance to such pleading.   I ask you, in short, gentlemen, for that
verdict of guilty which, in the circumstances, I regard you as,
unfortunately, bound to record.

[*Letting his eyes travel from the* JUDGE *and the jury to* FROME,
he sits down.

THE JUDGE.   [*Bending a little towards the jury, and speaking
in a business-like voice*] Members of the Jury, you have heard the
evidence, and the comments on it.   My only business is to make
clear to you the issues you have to try.   The facts are admitted,
so far as the alteration of this cheque and counterfoil by the

prisoner. The defence set up is that he was not in a responsible condition when he committed the crime. Well, you have heard the prisoner's story, and the evidence of the other witnesses—so far as it bears on the point of insanity. If you think that what you have heard establishes the fact that the prisoner was insane at the time of the forgery, you will find him guilty but insane. If, on the other hand, you conclude from what you have seen and heard that the prisoner was sane—and nothing short of insanity will count—you will find him guilty. In reviewing the testimony as to his mental condition you must bear in mind very carefully the evidence as to his demeanour and conduct both before and after the act of forgery—the evidence of the prisoner himself, of the woman, of the witness—er—Cokeson, and—er—of the cashier. And in regard to that I especially direct your attention to the prisoner's admission that the idea of adding the *ty* and the nought did come into his mind at the moment when the cheque was handed to him; and also to the alteration of the counterfoil, and to his subsequent conduct generally. The bearing of all this on the question of premeditation (and premeditation will imply sanity) is very obvious. You must not allow any considerations of age or temptation to weigh with you in the finding of your verdict. Before you can come to a verdict guilty but insane, you must be well and thoroughly convinced that the condition of his mind was such as would have qualified him at the moment for a lunatic asylum. [*He pauses; then, seeing that the jury are doubtful whether to retire or no, adds:*] You may retire, gentlemen, if you wish to do so.

[*The jury retire by a door behind the* JUDGE. *The* JUDGE *bends over his notes.* FALDER, *leaning from the dock, speaks excitedly to his solicitor, pointing down at* RUTH. *The solicitor in turn speaks to* FROME.

FROME. [*Rising*] My lord. The prisoner is very anxious that I should ask you if your lordship would kindly request the reporters not to disclose the name of the woman witness in the Press reports of these proceedings. Your lordship will understand that the consequences might be extremely serious to her.

THE JUDGE. [*Pointedly—with the suspicion of a smile*] Well, Mr. Frome, you deliberately took this course which involved bringing her here.

FROME. [*With an ironic bow*] If your lordship thinks I could have brought out the full facts in any other way?

THE JUDGE. H'm! Well.

FROME. There is very real danger to her, your lordship.

THE JUDGE. You see, I have to take your word for all that.

FROME. If your lordship would be so kind. I can assure your lordship that I am not exaggerating.

THE JUDGE. It goes very much against the grain with me that the name of a witness should ever be suppressed. [*With a glance at* FALDER, *who is gripping and clasping his hands before him, and then at* RUTH, *who is sitting perfectly rigid with her eyes fixed on* FALDER.] I'll consider your application. It must depend. I have to remember that she may have come here to commit perjury on the prisoner's behalf.

FROME. Your lordship, I really——

THE JUDGE. Yes, yes—I don't suggest anything of the sort, Mr. Frome. Leave it at that for the moment.

[*As he finishes speaking, the jury return, and file back into the box.*

CLERK OF ASSIZE. Members of the Jury, are you agreed on your verdict?

FOREMAN. We are.

CLERK OF ASSIZE. Is it Guilty, or Guilty but insane?

FOREMAN. Guilty.

[*The* JUDGE *nods; then, gathering up his notes, he looks at* FALDER, *who sits motionless.*

FROME. [*Rising*] If your lordship would allow me to address you in mitigation of sentence. I don't know if your lordship thinks I can add anything to what I have said to the jury on the score of the prisoner's youth, and the great stress under which he acted.

THE JUDGE. I don't think you can, Mr. Frome.

FROME. If your lordship says so—I do most earnestly beg your lordship to give the utmost weight to my plea. [*He sits down.*

THE JUDGE. [*To the Clerk*] Call upon him.

THE CLERK. Prisoner at the bar, you stand convicted of felony. Have you anything to say for yourself why the Court should not give you judgment according to Law?

[FALDER *shakes his head.*

THE JUDGE. William Falder, you have been given fair trial and found guilty, in my opinion rightly found guilty, of forgery. [*He pauses; then, consulting his notes, goes on.*] The defence was set up that you were not responsible for your actions at the moment of committing the crime. There is no doubt, I think, that this was a device to bring out at first hand the nature of the temptation to which you succumbed. For throughout the trial your counsel was in reality making an appeal for mercy. The setting up of this defence of course enabled him to put in some evidence that might weigh in that direction. Whether he was well advised to do so is another matter. He claimed that you should be treated rather as a patient than as a criminal. And this plea of his, which in the end amounted to a passionate appeal, he based in effect on an indictment of the march of Justice, which he practically accused of confirming and completing the process of criminality. Now, in considering how far I should allow weight to his appeal, I have a number of factors to take into account. I have to consider on the one hand the grave nature of your offence, the deliberate way in which you subsequently altered the counterfoil, the danger you caused to an innocent man—and that, to my mind, is a very grave point— and finally I have to consider the necessity of deterring others from following your example. On the other hand, I bear in mind that you are young, that you have hitherto borne a good character, that you were, if I am to believe your evidence and that of your witnesses, in a state of some emotional excitement when you committed this crime. I have every wish, consistently with my duty—not only to you, but to the community, to treat you with leniency. And this brings me to what are the determining factors in my mind in my consideration of your case. You are a clerk in a lawyer's office—that is a very serious aggravation in this case; no possible excuse can be made for you on the ground that you were not fully conversant with the nature of the crime you were committing and the penalties that attach to it.   It is said, however, that you were carried away by your emotions.   The story has been told here to-day of your relations with this—er—Mrs. Honeywill; on that story both the defence and the plea for mercy were in effect based.   Now what is that story ?   It is that you, a young man, and she a young woman unhappily married, had formed an attachment, which you both say—with what truth I am unable to gauge—had not yet resulted in immoral relations, but which you both admit was about to result in such relationship.   Your counsel has made an attempt to palliate this, on the ground that the woman is in what he describes, I think, as "a hopeless position."   As to that I can express no opinion.   She is a married woman, and the fact is patent that you committed this crime with the view of furthering an immoral design.   Now, however I might wish, I am not able to justify to my conscience a plea for mercy which has a basis inimical to morality.   It is vitiated *ab initio*.   Your counsel has made an attempt also to show that to punish you with further imprisonment would be unjust.   I do not follow him in these flights.   *The Law is what it is*—a majestic edifice, sheltering all of us, each stone of which rests on another.   I am concerned only with its administration.   The crime you have committed is a very serious one.   I cannot feel it in accordance with my duty to society to exercise the powers I have in your favour. You will go to penal servitude for three years.

[FALDER, *who throughout the* JUDGE'S *speech has looked at him steadily, lets his head fall forward on his breast.   RUTH starts up from her seat as he is taken out by the warders.   There is a bustle in court.*

THE JUDGE.   [*Speaking to the reporters*] Gentlemen of the Press, I think that the name of the female witness should not be reported.   [*The reporters bow their acquiescence.*

THE JUDGE.   [*To* RUTH, *who is staring in the direction in which* FALDER *has disappeared*] Do you understand, your name will not be mentioned?

COKESON. [*Pulling her sleeve*] The judge is speaking to you.

[RUTH *turns, stares at the* JUDGE, *and turns away.*

THE JUDGE. I shall sit rather late to-day. Call the next case.

CLERK OF ASSIZE. [*To a warder*] Put up John Booley.

[*To cries of* "Witnesses in the case of Booley"

The curtain falls.

ACT III

SCENE I

A prison. A plainly furnished room, with two large barred windows, overlooking the prisoners' exercise yard, where men, in yellow clothes marked with arrows, and yellow brimless caps, are seen in single file at a distance of four yards from each other walking rapidly on serpentine white lines marked on the concrete floor of the yard. Two warders in blue uniforms, with peaked caps and swords, are stationed amongst them. The room has distempered walls, a bookcase with numerous official-looking books, a cupboard between the windows, a plan of the prison on the wall, a writing-table covered with documents. It is Christmas Eve.

The GOVERNOR, *a neat, grave-looking man, with a trim, fair moustache, the eyes of a theorist, and grizzled hair, receding from the temples, is standing close to this writing-table looking at a sort of rough saw made out of a piece of metal. The hand in which he holds it is gloved, for two fingers are missing. The chief warder,* WOODER, *a tall, thin, military-looking man of sixty, with grey moustache and melancholy, monkey-like eyes, stands very upright two paces from him.*

THE GOVERNOR. [*With a faint, abstracted smile*] Queer-looking affair, Mr. Wooder! Where did you find it?

WOODER. In his mattress, sir. Haven't come across such a thing for two years now.

THE GOVERNOR. [*With curiosity*] Had he any set plan?

WOODER. He'd sawed his window-bar about that much. [*He holds up his thumb and finger a quarter of an inch apart.*]

THE GOVERNOR. I'll see him this afternoon. What's his name? Moaney! An old hand, I think?

WOODER. Yes, sir—fourth spell of penal. You'd think an

old lag like him would have had more sense by now. *[With pitying contempt.]* Occupied his mind, he said. Breaking in and breaking out—that's all they think about.

THE GOVERNOR. Who's next him?

WOODER. O'Cleary, sir.

THE GOVERNOR. The Irishman.

WOODER. Next him again there's that young fellow, Falder —star class—and next him old Clipton.

THE GOVERNOR. Ah, yes! "The philosopher." I want to see him about his eyes.

WOODER. Curious thing, sir: they seem to know when there's one of these tries at escape going on. It makes them restive—there's a regular wave going through them just now.

THE GOVERNOR. *[Meditatively]* Odd things—those waves. *[Turning to look at the prisoners exercising.]* Seem quiet enough out here!

WOODER. That Irishman, O'Cleary, began banging on his door this morning. Little thing like that's quite enough to upset the whole lot. They're just like dumb animals at times.

THE GOVERNOR. I've seen it with horses before thunder— it'll run right through cavalry lines.

[The prison CHAPLAIN *has entered. He is a dark-haired, ascetic man, in clerical undress, with a peculiarly steady, tight-lipped face and slow, cultured speech.*

THE GOVERNOR. *[Holding up the saw]* Seen this, Miller?

THE CHAPLAIN. Useful-looking specimen.

THE GOVERNOR. Do for the Museum, eh! *[He goes to the cupboard and opens it, displaying to view a number of quaint ropes, hooks, and metal tools with labels tied on them.]* That'll do, thanks, Mr. Wooder.

WOODER. *[Saluting]* Thank you, sir.   *[He goes out.*

THE GOVERNOR. Account for the state of the men last day or two, Miller? Seems going through the whole place.

THE CHAPLAIN. No. I don't know of anything.

THE GOVERNOR. By the way, will you dine with us to-morrow?

THE CHAPLAIN.   Christmas Day? Thanks very much.

THE GOVERNOR.   Worries me to feel the men discontented. [*Gazing at the saw.*] Have to punish this poor devil. Can't help liking a man who tries to escape.

[*He places the saw in his pocket and locks the cupboard again.*

THE CHAPLAIN.   Extraordinary perverted will-power— some of them. Nothing to be done till it's broken.

THE GOVERNOR.   And not much afterwards, I'm afraid. Ground too hard for golf?   [WOODER *comes in again.*

WOODER.   Visitor to speak to you, sir. I told him it wasn't usual.

THE GOVERNOR.   What about?

WOODER.   Shall I put him off, sir?

THE GOVERNOR.   [*Resignedly*] No, no. Let's see him. Don't go, Miller.

[WOODER *motions to someone without, and as the visitor comes in withdraws.*

[*The visitor is* COKESON, *who is attired in a thick overcoat to the knees, woollen gloves, and carries a top hat.*

COKESON.   I'm sorry to trouble you. But it's about a young man you've got here.

THE GOVERNOR.   We have a good many.

COKESON.   Name of Falder, forgery. [*Producing a card, and handing it to the* GOVERNOR.] Firm of James and Walter How. Well known in the law.

THE GOVERNOR.   [*Receiving the card—with a faint smile.*] What do you want to see me about, sir?

COKESON.   [*Suddenly seeing the prisoners at exercise*] Why! what a sight!

THE GOVERNOR.   Yes, we have that privilege from here; my office is being done up. [*Sitting down at his table.*] Now, please!

COKESON.   [*Dragging his eyes with difficulty from the window*] I *wanted* to say a word to you; I shan't keep you long. [*Confidentially*] Fact is, I oughtn't to be here by rights. His sister came to me—he's got no father and mother—and she was in some distress. "My husband won't let me go and see him," she said; "says he's disgraced the family. And his other sister," she said, "is an invalid." And she asked me to come. Well, I take an interest in him. He was our junior—I go to the same chapel—and I didn't like to refuse.

THE GOVERNOR. I'm afraid he's not allowed a visitor yet—he's only here for his one month's separate confinement.

COKESON. You see, I saw him while he was shut up waiting for his trial and he was lonely.

THE GOVERNOR. [*With faint amusement*] Ring the bell—would you, Miller. [*To* COKESON] You'd like to hear what the doctor says about him, perhaps.

THE CHAPLAIN. [*Ringing the bell*] You are not accustomed to prisons, it would seem, sir.

COKESON. No. But it's a pitiful sight. He's quite a young fellow. I said to him: "Be patient," I said. "Patient!" he said. "A day," he said, "shut up in your cell thinking and brooding as I do, it's longer than a year outside, I can't help it," he said; "I try—but I'm built that way, Mr. Cokeson." And he held his hand up to his face. I could see the tears trickling through his fingers. It wasn't nice.

THE CHAPLAIN. He's a young man with rather peculiar eyes, isn't he? Not Church of England, I think?

COKESON. No.

THE CHAPLAIN. I know.

THE GOVERNOR. [*To* WOODER, *who has come in*] Ask the doctor to be good enough to come here for a minute. [WOODER *salutes, and goes out.*] Let's see, he's not married?

COKESON. No. [*Confidentially*] But there's a party he's very much attached to, not altogether com-il-fo. It's a sad story.

THE CHAPLAIN. If it wasn't for drink and women, sir, this prison might be closed.

COKESON. [*Looking at the* CHAPLAIN *over his spectacles*] Ye-es, but I wanted to tell you about that, special. It preys on his mind.

THE GOVERNOR. Well!

COKESON. Like this. The woman had a nahsty, spiteful

feller for a husband, and she'd left him. Fact is, she was going away with our young friend. It's not nice—but I've looked over it. Well, after the trial she said she'd earn her living apart, and wait for him to come out. That was a great consolation to him. But after a month she came to me—I *don't* know her personally—and she said: "I can't earn the children's living, let alone my own—I've got no friends. I'm obliged to keep out of everybody's way, else my husband'd get to know where I was. I'm very much reduced," she said. And she has lost flesh. "I'll have to go in the workhouse!" It's a painful story. I said to her: "No," I said, "not that! I've got a wife an' family, but sooner than you should do that I'll spare you a little myself." "Really," she said—she's a nice creature—"I don't like to take it from you. I think I'd better go back to my husband." Well, I know he's a nahsty, spiteful feller—drinks—but I didn't like to persuade her not to.

THE CHAPLAIN. Surely, no.

COKESON. Ye-es, but I'm sorry now. He's got his three years to serve. I *want* things to be pleasant for him.

THE CHAPLAIN. [*With a touch of impatience*] The Law hardly shares your view, I'm afraid.

COKESON. He's all alone there by himself. I'm afraid it'll turn him silly. And nobody wants that, I s'pose. He cried when I saw him. I don't like to see a man cry.

THE CHAPLAIN. It's a very rare thing for them to give way like that.

COKESON. [*Looking at him—in a tone of sudden dogged hostility*] I keep dogs.

THE CHAPLAIN. Indeed?

COKESON. Ye-es. And I say this: I wouldn't shut one of them up all by himself, week after week, not if he'd bit me all over.

THE CHAPLAIN. Unfortunately, the criminal is not a dog; he has a sense of right and wrong.

COKESON. But that's not the way to make him feel it.

THE CHAPLAIN. Ah! there I'm afraid we must differ.

COKESON. It's the same with dogs. If you treat 'em with

kindness they'll do anything for you; but to shut 'em up alone, it only makes 'em savage.

THE CHAPLAIN. Surely you should allow those who have had a little more experience than yourself to know what is best for prisoners.

COKESON. [*Doggedly*] I know this young feller, I've watched him for years. He's eurotic—got no stamina. His father died of consumption. I'm thinking of his future. If he's to be kept there shut up by himself, without a cat to keep him company, it'll do him harm. I said to him: "Where do you feel it?" "I can't tell you, Mr. Cokeson," he said, "but sometimes I could beat my head against the wall." It's not nice.

[*During this speech the* DOCTOR *has entered. He is a medium-sized, rather good-looking man, with a quick eye. He stands leaning against the window.*

THE GOVERNOR. This gentleman thinks the separate is telling on Q 3007—Falder, young thin fellow, star class. What do you say, Doctor Clements?

THE DOCTOR. He doesn't like it, but it's not doing him any harm, it's only a month.

COKESON. But he was weeks before he came in here.

THE DOCTOR. We can always tell. He's lost no weight since he's been here.

COKESON. It's his state of mind I'm speaking of.

THE DOCTOR. His mind's all right so far. He's nervous, rather melancholy. I don't see signs of anything more. I'm watching him carefully.

COKESON. [*Nonplussed*] I'm glad to hear you say that.

THE CHAPLAIN. [*More suavely*] It's just at this period that we are able to make some impression on them, sir. I am speaking from my special standpoint.

COKESON. [*Turning bewildered to the* GOVERNOR] I *don't* want to be unpleasant, but I do feel it's awkward.

THE GOVERNOR. I'll make a point of seeing him to-day.

COKESON. I'm much obliged to you. I thought perhaps seeing him every day you wouldn't notice it.

THE GOVERNOR. [*Rather sharply*] If any sign of injury to his health shows itself his case will be reported at once. That's fully provided for.   [*He rises.*

COKESON. [*Following his own thoughts*] Of course, what you don't see doesn't trouble you; but I don't want to have him on my mind.

THE GOVERNOR. I think you may safely leave it to us, sir.

COKESON. [*Mollified and apologetic*] I thought you'd understand me. I'm a plain man—never set myself up against authority. [*Expanding to the* CHAPLAIN.] Nothing personal meant. *Good*-morning.

[*As he goes out the three officials do not look at each other, but their faces wear peculiar expressions.*

THE CHAPLAIN. Our friend seems to think that prison is a hospital.

COKESON. [*Returning suddenly with an apologetic air*] There's just one little thing. This woman—I suppose I mustn't ask you to let him see her. It'd be a rare treat for them both. He'll be thinking about her all the time. Of course she's not his wife. But he's quite safe in here. They're a pitiful couple. You couldn't make an exception?

THE GOVERNOR. [*Wearily*] As you say, my dear sir, I couldn't make an exception; he won't be allowed a visit till he goes to a convict prison.

COKESON. I see. [*Rather coldly.*] Sorry to have troubled you.
                                    [*He again goes out.*

THE CHAPLAIN. [*Shrugging his shoulders*] The plain man indeed, poor fellow. Come and have some lunch, Clements?
                                    [*He and the* DOCTOR *go out talking.*

[*The* GOVERNOR, *with a sigh, sits down at his table and takes up a pen.*

The curtain falls.

SCENE II

Part of the ground corridor of the prison.   The walls are coloured with greenish distemper up to a stripe of deeper green about the height of a man's shoulder, and above this line are whitewashed. The floor is of blackened stones.   Daylight is filtering through a heavily barred window at the end.   The doors of four cells are visible.   Each cell door has a little round peep-hole at the level of a man's eye, covered by a little round disc, which, raised upwards, affords a view of the cell.   On the wall, close to each cell door, hangs a little square board with the prisoner's name, number, and record.

Overhead can be seen the iron structures of the first-floor and second-floor corridors.

The WARDER INSTRUCTOR, *a bearded man in blue uniform, with an apron, and some dangling keys, is just emerging from one of the cells.*

INSTRUCTOR.   [*Speaking from the door into the cell*] I'll have another bit for you when that's finished.

O'CLEARY.   [*Unseen—in an Irish voice*] Little doubt o' that, sirr.

INSTRUCTOR.   [*Gossiping*] Well, you'd rather have it than nothing, I s'pose.

O'CLEARY.   An' that's the blessed truth.

[*Sounds are heard of a cell door being closed and locked, and of approaching footsteps.*

INSTRUCTOR.   [*In a sharp, changed voice*] Look alive over it!

[*He shuts the cell door, and stands at attention.*

[*The* GOVERNOR *comes walking down the corridor, followed by* WOODER.

THE GOVERNOR.   Anything to report?

INSTRUCTOR.   [*Saluting*] Q 3007 [*He points to a cell*] is behind with his work, sir.   He'll lose marks to-day.

[*The* GOVERNOR *nods and passes on to the end cell.   The* INSTRUCTOR *goes away.*

THE GOVERNOR.   This is our maker of saws, isn't it?

[*He takes the saw from his pocket as* WOODER *throws open the door of the cell. The convict* MOANEY *is seen lying on his bed, athwart the cell, with his cap on. He springs up and stands in the middle of the cell. He is a raw-boned fellow, about fifty-six years old, with outstanding bat's ears and fierce, staring, steel-coloured eyes.*

WOODER.   Cap off! [MOANEY *removes his cap.*]   Out here!
                                      [MOANEY *comes to the door.*

THE GOVERNOR.   [*Beckoning him out into the corridor, and holding up the saw—with the manner of an officer speaking to a private*] Anything to say about this, my man? [MOANEY *is silent.*]   Come!

MOANEY.   It passed the time.

THE GOVERNOR.   [*Pointing into the cell*] Not enough to do, eh?

MOANEY.   It don't occupy your mind.

THE GOVERNOR.   [*Tapping the saw*] You might find a better way than this.

MOANEY.   [*Sullenly*] Well! What way! I must keep my hand in against the time I get out. What's the good of anything else to me at my time of life? [*With a gradual change to civility, as his tongue warms.*] Ye know that, sir. I'll be in again within a year or two, after I've done this lot. I don't want to disgrace meself when I'm out. *You've* got your pride keeping the prison smart; well, I've got mine. [*Seeing that the* GOVERNOR *is listening with interest, he goes on, pointing to the saw.*] I *must* be doin' a little o' this. It's no harm to any one. I was five weeks makin' that saw—a bit of all right it is, too; now I'll get cells, I suppose, or seven days' bread and water. You can't help it, sir, I know that—I quite put meself in your place.

THE GOVERNOR.   Now, look here, Moaney, if I pass it over will you give me your word not to try it on again? Think!

[*He goes into the cell, walks to the end of it, mounts the stool, and tries the window-bars.*

THE GOVERNOR.   [*Returning*] Well?

MOANEY. [*Who has been reflecting*] I've got another six weeks to do in here, alone. I can't do it and think o' nothing. I must have something to interest me. You've made me a sporting offer, sir, but I can't pass my word about it. I shouldn't like to deceive a gentleman. [*Pointing into the cell*] Another four hours' steady work would have done it.

THE GOVERNOR. Yes, and what then? Caught, brought back, punishment. Five weeks' hard work to make this, and cells at the end of it, while they put a new bar to your window. Is it worth it, Moaney?

MOANEY. [*With a sort of fierceness*] Yes, it is.

THE GOVERNOR. [*Putting his hand to his brow*] Oh, well! Two days' cells—bread and water.

MOANEY. Thank 'e, sir.

[*He turns quickly like an animal and slips into his cell.*]
[*The* GOVERNOR *looks after him and shakes his head as* WOODER *closes and locks the cell door.*]

THE GOVERNOR. Open Clipton's cell.

[WOODER *opens the door of* CLIPTON'S *cell.* CLIPTON *is sitting on a stool just inside the door, at work on a pair of trousers. He is a small, thick, oldish man, with an almost shaven head, and smouldering little dark eyes behind smoked spectacles. He gets up and stands motionless in the doorway, peering at his visitors.*]

THE GOVERNOR. [*Beckoning*] Come out here a minute, Clipton.

[CLIPTON, *with a sort of dreadful quietness, comes into the corridor, the needle and thread in his hand. The* GOVERNOR *signs to* WOODER, *who goes into the cell and inspects it carefully.*]

THE GOVERNOR. How are your eyes?

CLIPTON. I don't complain of them. I don't see the sun here. [*He makes a stealthy movement, protruding his neck a little.*] There's just one thing, Mr. Governor, as you're speaking to me. I wish you'd ask the cove next door here to keep a bit quieter.

THE GOVERNOR. What's the matter? I don't want any tales, Clipton.

CLIPTON. He keeps me awake. I don't know who he is.

[*With contempt*] One of this *star* class, I expect.   Oughtn't to be here with *us*.

THE GOVERNOR.   [*Quietly*] Quite right, Clipton.   He'll be moved when there's a cell vacant.

CLIPTON.   He knocks about like a wild beast in the early morning.   I'm not used to it—stops me getting my sleep out. In the evening too.   It's not fair, Mr. Governor, as you're speaking to me.   Sleep's the comfort I've got here; I'm entitled to take it out full.

[WOODER *comes out of the cell, and instantly, as though extinguished,* CLIPTON *moves with stealthy suddenness back into his cell.*

WOODER.   All right, sir.

[*The* GOVERNOR *nods.   The door is closed and locked.*

THE GOVERNOR.   Which is the man who banged on his door this morning?

WOODER.   [*Going towards* O'CLEARY'S *cell*] This one, sir; O'Cleary.   [*He lifts the disc and glances through the peep-hole.*

THE GOVERNOR.   Open.

[WOODER *throws open the door.* O'CLEARY, *who is seated at a little table by the door as if listening, springs up and stands at attention just inside the doorway.   He is a broad-faced, middle-aged man, with a wide, thin, flexible mouth, and little holes under his high cheek-bones.*

THE GOVERNOR.   Where's the joke, O'Cleary?

O'CLEARY.   The joke, your honour?   I've not seen one for a long time.

THE GOVERNOR.   Banging on your door?

O'CLEARY.   Oh! that!

THE GOVERNOR.   It's womanish.

O'CLEARY.   An' it's that I'm becoming this two months past.

THE GOVERNOR.   Anything to complain of?

O'CLEARY.   No, sirr.

THE GOVERNOR.   You're an old hand; you ought to know better.

O'CLEARY.   Yes, I've been through it all.

THE GOVERNOR. You've got a youngster next door; you'll upset him.

O'CLEARY. It cam' over me, your honour. I can't always be the same steady man.

THE GOVERNOR. Work all right?

O'CLEARY. [*Taking up a rush mat he is making*] Oh! I can do it on my head. It's the miserablest stuff—don't take the brains of a mouse. [*Working his mouth.*] It's here I feel it— the want of a little noise—a terrible little wud aise me.

THE GOVERNOR. You know as well as I do that if you were out in the shops you wouldn't be allowed to talk.

O'CLEARY. [*With a look of profound meaning*] Not with my mouth.

THE GOVERNOR. Well, then?

O'CLEARY. But it's the great conversation I'd be havin'.

THE GOVERNOR. [*With a smile*] Well, no more conversation on your door.

O'CLEARY. No, sirr, I wud not have the little wit to repate meself.

THE GOVERNOR. [*Turning*] Good-night.

O'CLEARY. Good-night, your honour.

[*He turns into his cell. The* GOVERNOR *shuts the door.*]

THE GOVERNOR. [*Looking at the record card*] Can't help liking the poor blackguard.

WOODER. He's an amiable man, sir.

THE GOVERNOR. [*Pointing down the corridor*] Ask the doctor to come here, Mr. Wooder.

[WOODER *salutes and goes away down the corridor.*
[*The* GOVERNOR *goes to the door of* FALDER'S *cell. He raises his uninjured hand to uncover the peep-hole; but, without uncovering it, shakes his head and drops his hand; then, after scrutinizing the record board, he opens the cell door.* FALDER, *who is standing against it, lurches forward, with a gasp.*]

THE GOVERNOR. [*Beckoning him out*] Now tell me; can't you settle down, Falder?

FALDER. [*In a breathless voice*] Yes, sir.

THE GOVERNOR. You know what I mean? It's no good running your head against a stone wall, is it?

FALDER. No, sir.

THE GOVERNOR. Well, come.

FALDER. I try, sir.

THE GOVERNOR. Can't you sleep?

FALDER. Very little. Between two o'clock and getting up's the worst time.

THE GOVERNOR. How's that?

FALDER. [*His lips twitch with a sort of smile*] I don't know, sir. I was always nervous. [*Suddenly voluble.*] Everything seems to get such a size then. I feel I'll never get out as long as I live.

THE GOVERNOR. That's morbid, my lad. Pull yourself together.

FALDER. [*With an equally sudden dogged resentment*] Yes— I've got to——

THE GOVERNOR. Think of all these other fellows.

FALDER. They're used to it.

THE GOVERNOR. They all had to go through it once for the first time, just as you're doing now.

FALDER. Yes, sir, I shall get to be like them in time, I suppose.

THE GOVERNOR. [*Rather taken aback*] H'm! Well! That rests with you. Now, come. Set your mind to it, like a good fellow. You're still quite young. A man can make himself what he likes.

FALDER. [*Wistfully*] Yes, sir.

THE GOVERNOR. Take a good hold of yourself. Do you read?

FALDER. I don't take the words in. [*Hanging his head.*] I know it's no good; but I can't help thinking of what's going on outside.

THE GOVERNOR. Private trouble?

FALDER. Yes.

THE GOVERNOR. You mustn't think about it.

FALDER. [*Looking back at his cell*] How can I help it, sir?

[*He suddenly becomes motionless as* WOODER *and the* DOCTOR *approach. The* GOVERNOR *motions to him to go back into his cell.*

FALDER. [*Quick and low*] I'm quite right in my head, sir.

[*He goes back into his cell.*

THE GOVERNOR. [*To the* DOCTOR] Just go in and see him, Clements.

[*The* DOCTOR *goes into the cell. The* GOVERNOR *pushes the door to, nearly closing it, and walks towards the window.*

WOODER. [*Following*] Sorry you should be troubled like this, sir. Very contented lot of men, on the whole.

THE GOVERNOR. [*Shortly*] You think so?

WOODER. Yes, sir. It's Christmas doing it, in my opinion.

THE GOVERNOR. [*To himself*] Queer, that!

WOODER. Beg pardon, sir?

THE GOVERNOR. Christmas!

[*He turns towards the window, leaving* WOODER *looking at him with a sort of pained anxiety.*

WOODER. [*Suddenly*] Do you think we make show enough, sir? If you'd like us to have more holly?

THE GOVERNOR. Not at all, Mr. Wooder.

WOODER. Very good, sir.

[*The* DOCTOR *has come out of* FALDER'S *cell, and the* GOVERNOR *beckons to him.*

THE GOVERNOR. Well?

THE DOCTOR. I can't make anything much of him. He's nervous, of course.

THE GOVERNOR. Is there any sort of case to report? Quite frankly, Doctor.

THE DOCTOR. Well, I don't think the separate's doing him any good; but then I could say the same of a lot of them—they'd get on better in the shops, there's no doubt.

THE GOVERNOR. You mean you'd have to recommend others?

THE DOCTOR. A dozen at least. It's on his nerves. There's nothing tangible. This fellow here [*pointing to* O'CLEARY'S *cell*], for instance—feels it just as much, in his way. If I once get away from physical facts—I shan't know where I am. Conscientiously, sir, I don't know how to differentiate him. He hasn't lost weight. Nothing wrong with his eyes. His pulse is good. Talks all right. It's only another week before he goes.

THE GOVERNOR. It doesn't amount to melancholia?

THE DOCTOR. [*Shaking his head*] I can report on him if you like; but if I do I ought to report on others.

THE GOVERNOR. I see. [*Looking towards* FALDER'S *cell.*] The poor devil must just stick it then.

[*As he says this he looks absently at* WOODER.

WOODER. Beg pardon, sir?

[*For answer the* GOVERNOR *stares at him, turns on his heel, and walks away.* [*There is a sound as of beating on metal.*

THE GOVERNOR. [*Stopping*] Mr. Wooder?

WOODER. Banging on his door, sir. I thought we should have more of that.

[*He hurries forward, passing the* GOVERNOR, *who follows slowly.*

The curtain falls.

SCENE III

FALDER'S *cell, a whitewashed space thirteen feet broad by seven deep, and nine feet high, with a rounded ceiling. The floor is of shiny blackened bricks. The barred window, with a ventilator, is high up in the middle of the end wall. In the middle of the opposite end wall is the narrow door. In a corner are the mattress and bedding rolled up (two blankets, two sheets, and a coverlet). Above them is a quarter-circular wooden shelf, on which is a Bible and several little devotional books, piled in a symmetrical pyramid; there are also a black hair-brush, tooth-brush, and a bit of soap. In another corner is the wooden frame of a bed, standing on end. There is a dark ventilator under the window, and another over the door.* FALDER'S *work (a shirt to which he is putting button-holes) is hung to a nail on the wall over a small wooden table, on which the novel " Lorna Doone" lies open. Low down in the corner by the door is a thick glass screen, about a foot square, covering the gas-jet let into the wall. There is also a wooden stool, and a pair of shoes beneath it. Three bright round tins are set under the window.*

In fast-failing daylight, FALDER, in his stockings, is seen standing *motionless, with his head inclined towards the door, listening. He moves a little closer to the door, his stockinged feet making no noise. He stops at the door. He is trying harder and harder to hear something, any little thing that is going on outside. He springs suddenly upright—as if at a sound—and remains perfectly motionless. Then, with a heavy sigh, he moves to his work, and stands looking at it, with his head down; he does a stitch or two, having the air of a man so lost in sadness that each stitch is, as it were, a coming to life. Then, turning abruptly, he begins pacing the cell, moving his head, like an animal pacing its cage. He stops again at the door, listens, and, placing the palms of his hands against it with his fingers spread out, leans his forehead against the iron. Turning from it presently, he moves slowly back towards the window tracing his way with his finger along the top line of the distemper that runs round the walls. He stops under the window, and, picking up the lid of one of the tins, peers into it, as if trying to make a companion of his own face. It has grown very nearly dark. Suddenly the lid falls out of his hand with a clatter—the only sound that has broken the silence— and he stands staring intently at the wall where the stuff of the shirt is hanging rather white in the darkness—he seems to be seeing somebody or something there. There is a sharp tap and click; the cell light behind the glass screen has been turned up. The cell is brightly lighted. FALDER is seen gasping for breath. A sound from far away, as of distant, dull beating on thick metal, is suddenly audible. FALDER shrinks back, not able to bear this sudden clamour. But the sound grows, as though some great tumbril were rolling towards the cell. And gradually it seems to hypnotize him. He begins creeping inch by inch nearer to the* door. *The banging sound, travelling from cell to cell, draws closer and closer;* FALDER'S *hands are seen moving as if his spirit had already joined in this beating, and the sound swells till it seems to have entered the very cell. He suddenly raises his clenched fists. Panting violently, he flings himself at his door, and beats on it.*

The curtain falls.

ACT IV

The scene is again COKESON'S *room, at a few minutes to ten of a
March morning, two years later. The doors are all open.*
SWEEDLE, *now blessed with a sprouting moustache, is getting
the offices ready. He arranges papers on* COKESON'S *table;
then goes to a covered washstand, raises the lid, and looks at
himself in the mirror. While he is gazing his fill* RUTH
HONEYWILL *comes in through the outer office and stands in the
doorway. There seems a kind of exultation and excitement
behind her habitual impassivity.*

SWEEDLE. [*Suddenly seeing her, and dropping the lid of the
washstand with a bang*] Hello! It's you!
RUTH. Yes.
SWEEDLE. There's only me here! They don't waste their
time hurrying down in the morning. Why, it must be two years
since we had the pleasure of seeing you. [*Nervously*] What
have you been doing with yourself?
RUTH. [*Sardonically*] Living.
SWEEDLE. [*Impressed*] If you want to see *him* [*he points to*
COKESON'S *chair*], he'll be here directly—never misses—not
much. [*Delicately*] I hope our friend's back from the country.
His time's been up these three months, if I remember. [RUTH
nods.] I was awful sorry about that. The governor made a
mistake—if you ask me.
RUTH. He did.
SWEEDLE. He ought to have given him a chanst. And, *I* say,
the judge ought to ha' let him go after that. They've forgot
what human nature's like. Whereas *we* know.
[RUTH *gives him a honeyed smile.*
SWEEDLE. They come down on you like a cartload of bricks,
flatten you out, and when you don't swell up again they com-

61

plain of it.   I know 'em—seen a lot of that sort of thing in my
time.   [*He shakes his head in the plenitude of wisdom.*]   Why,
only the other day the governor——

[*But* COKESON *has come in through the outer office; brisk with
east wind, and decidedly greyer.*

COKESON.   [*Drawing off his coat and gloves*] Why! it's you!
[*Then motioning* SWEEDLE *out, and closing the door*] Quite a
stranger!   Must be two years.   D'you want to see me?   I can
give you a minute.   Sit down!   Family well?

RUTH.   Yes.   I'm not living where I was.

COKESON.   [*Eyeing her askance*] I hope things are more
comfortable at home.

RUTH.   I couldn't stay with Honeywill, after all.

COKESON.   You haven't done anything rash, I hope.   I
should be sorry if you'd done anything rash.

RUTH.   I've kept the children with me.

COKESON.   [*Beginning to feel that things are not so jolly as he
had hoped*] Well, I'm glad to have seen you.   You've not heard
from the young man, I suppose, since he came out?

RUTH.   Yes, I ran across him yesterday.

COKESON.   I hope he's well.

RUTH.   [*With sudden fierceness*] He can't get anything to do.
It's dreadful to see him.   He's just skin and bone.

COKESON.   [*With genuine concern*] Dear me!   I'm sorry to
hear that.   [*On his guard again*] Didn't they find him a place
when his time was up?

RUTH.   He was only there three weeks.   It got out.

COKESON.   I'm sure I don't know what I can do for you.
I don't like to be snubby.

RUTH.   I can't bear his being like that.

COKESON.   [*Scanning her not unprosperous figure*] I know his
relations aren't very forthy about him.   Perhaps *you* can do
something for him, till he finds his feet.

RUTH.   Not now.   I could have—but not *now*.

COKESON.   I don't understand.

RUTH.   [*Proudly*] I've seen *him* again—that's all over.

COKESON. [*Staring at her—disturbed*] I'm a family man—
I don't want to hear anything unpleasant. Excuse me—I'm
very busy.

RUTH. I'd have gone home to my people in the country long
ago, but they've never got over me marrying Honeywill. I
never was waywise, Mr. Cokeson, but I'm proud. I was only
a girl, you see, when I married him. I thought the world of
him, of course . . . he used to come travelling to our farm.

COKESON. [*Regretfully*] I did hope you'd have got on better,
after you saw me.

RUTH. He used me worse than ever. He couldn't break my
nerve, but I lost my health; and then he began knocking the
children about. . . . I couldn't stand that. I wouldn't go back
now, if he were dying.

COKESON. [*Who has risen and is shifting about as though
dodging a stream of lava*] We mustn't be violent, must we?

RUTH. [*Smouldering*] A man that can't behave better than
that—————   [*There is silence.*

COKESON. [*Fascinated in spite of himself*] Then there you
were! And what did you do then?

RUTH. [*With a shrug*] Tried the same as when I left him
before . . . making shirts . . . cheap things. It was the best I
could get, but I never made more then ten shillings a week,
buying my own cotton and working all day; I hardly ever got
to bed till past twelve. I kept at it for nine months. [*Fiercely*]
Well, I'm not fit for that; I wasn't made for it. I'd rather die.

COKESON. My dear woman! We mustn't talk like that.

RUTH. It was starvation for the children too—after what
they'd always had. I soon got not to care. I used to be too tired.
                              [*She is silent.*

COKESON. [*With fearful curiosity*] And—what happened
then?

RUTH. [*With a laugh*] My employer happened then—he's
happened ever since.

COKESON. Dear! Oh dear! I never came across a thing like
this.

RUTH. [*Dully*] He's treated me all right. But I've done with that. [*Suddenly her lips begin to quiver, and she hides them with the back of her hand.*] I never thought I'd see *him* again, you see. It was just a chance I met him by Hyde Park. We went in there and sat down, and he told me all about himself. Oh! Mr. Cokeson, give him another chance.

COKESON. [*Greatly disturbed*] Then you've both lost your livings! What a horrible position!

RUTH. If he could only get here—where there's nothing to find out about him!

COKESON. We can't have anything derogative to the firm.

RUTH. I've no one else to go to.

COKESON. I'll speak to the partners, but I don't think they'll take him, under the circumstances. I don't really.

RUTH. He came with me; he's down there in the street.
                              [*She points to the window.*

COKESON. [*On his dignity*] He shouldn't have done that until he's sent for. [*Then softening at the look on her face*] We've got a vacancy, as it happens, but I can't promise anything.

RUTH. It would be the saving of him.

COKESON. Well, I'll do what I can, but I'm not sanguine. Now tell him that I don't want him here till I see how things are. Leave your address? [*Repeating her.*] 83, Mullingar Street? [*He notes it on blotting-paper.*] Good-morning.

RUTH. Thank you. [*She moves towards the door, turns as if to speak but does not, and goes away.*

COKESON. [*Wiping his head and forehead with a large white cotton handkerchief*] What a business! [*Then, looking amongst his papers, he sounds his bell. SWEEDLE answers it.*]

COKESON. Was that young Richards coming here to-day after the clerk's place?

SWEEDLE. Yes.

COKESON. Well, keep him in the air; I don't want to see him yet.

SWEEDLE. What shall I tell him, sir?

COKESON. [*With asperity*] Invent something. Use your brains. Don't stump him off altogether.

SWEEDLE. Shall I tell him that we've got illness, sir?

COKESON. No! Nothing untrue. Say I'm not here to-day.

SWEEDLE. Yes, sir. Keep him hankering?

COKESON. Exactly. And look here. You remember Falder? I may be having him round to see me. Now, treat him like you'd have him treat you in a similar position.

SWEEDLE. I naturally should do.

COKESON. That's right. When a man's down never hit 'im. 'Tisn't necessary. Give him a hand up. That's a metaphor I recommend to you in life. It's sound policy.

SWEEDLE. Do you think the governors will take him on again, sir?

COKESON. Can't say anything about that. [*At the sound of someone having entered the outer office*] Who's there?

SWEEDLE. [*Going to the door and looking*] It's Falder, sir.

COKESON. [*Vexed*] Dear me! That's very naughty of her. Tell him to call again. I don't want——

[*He breaks off as* FALDER *comes in.* FALDER *is thin, pale, older, his eyes have grown more restless. His clothes are very worn and loose.* [SWEEDLE, *nodding cheerfully, withdraws.*

COKESON. Glad to see you. You're rather previous. [*Trying to keep things pleasant.*] Shake hands! She's striking while the iron's hot. [*He wipes his forehead.*] I don't blame her. She's anxious.

[FALDER *timidly takes* COKESON's *hand and glances towards the partners' door.*

COKESON. No—not yet! Sit down! [FALDER *sits in the chair at the side of* COKESON's *table, on which he places his cap.*] Now you are here I'd like you to give me a little account of yourself. [*Looking at him over his spectacles.*] How's your health?

FALDER. I'm alive, Mr. Cokeson.

COKESON. [*Preoccupied*] I'm glad to hear that. About this matter. I don't like doing anything out of the ordinary; it's not my habit. I'm a plain man, and I want everything smooth and straight. But I promised your friend to speak to the partners, and I always keep my word.

FALDER. I just want a chance, Mr. Cokeson. I've paid for that job a thousand times and more. I have, sir. No one knows. They say I weighed more when I came out than when I went in. They couldn't weigh me here [*he touches his head*] or here [*he touches his heart, and gives a sort of laugh*]. Till last night I'd thought there was nothing in here at all.

COKESON. [*Concerned*] You've not got heart disease?

FALDER. Oh! they passed me sound enough.

COKESON. But they got you a place, didn't they?

FALDER. Yes; very good people, knew all about it—very kind to me. I thought I was going to get on first-rate. But one day, all of a sudden, the other clerks got wind of it. . . . I couldn't stick it, Mr. Cokeson, I couldn't, sir.

COKESON. Easy, my dear fellow, easy.

FALDER. I had one small job after that, but it didn't last.

COKESON. How was that?

FALDER. It's no good deceiving you, Mr. Cokeson. The fact is, I seem to be struggling against a thing that's all round me. I can't explain it: it's as if I was in a net; as fast as I cut it here, it grows up there. I didn't act as I ought to have, about references; but what are you to do? You must have them. And that made me afraid, and I left. In fact, I'm—I'm afraid all the time now.

[*He bows his head and leans dejectedly silent over the table.*

COKESON. I feel for you—I do really. Aren't your sisters going to do anything for you?

FALDER. One's in consumption. And the other——

COKESON. Ye . . . es. She told me her husband wasn't quite pleased with you.

FALDER. When I went there—they were at supper—my sister wanted to give me a kiss—I know. But he just looked at her, and said: "What have you come for?" Well, I pocketed my pride and I said: "Aren't you going to give me your hand,

Jim? Cis is, I know," I said. "Look here!" he said, "that's all very well, but we'd better come to an understanding. I've been expecting you, and I've made up my mind. I'll give you twenty-five pounds to go to Canada with." "I see," I said—"good riddance! No, thanks; keep your twenty-five pounds." Friendship's a queer thing when you've been where I have.

COKESON. I understand. Will you take the twenty-five pound from me? [*Flustered, as* FALDER *regards him with a queer smile.*] Quite without prejudice; I meant it kindly.

FALDER. They wouldn't let me in.

COKESON. Oh! Ah! No! You aren't looking the thing.

FALDER. I've slept in the Park three nights this week. The dawns aren't all poetry there. But meeting her—I feel a different man this morning. I've often thought the being fond of her's the best thing about me; it's sacred, somehow—and yet it did for me. That's queer, isn't it?

COKESON. I'm sure we're all very sorry for you.

FALDER. That's what I've found, Mr. Cokeson. Awfully sorry for me. [*With quiet bitterness*] But it doesn't do to associate with criminals!

COKESON. Come, come, it's no use calling yourself names. That never did a man any good. Put a face on it.

FALDER. It's easy enough to put a face on it, sir, when you're independent. Try it when you're down like me. They talk about giving you your deserts. Well, I think I've had just a bit over.

COKESON. [*Eyeing him askance over his spectacles*] I hope they haven't made a Socialist of you.

[FALDER *is suddenly still, as if brooding over his past self; he utters a peculiar laugh.*

COKESON. You must give them credit for the best intentions. Really you must. Nobody wishes you harm, I'm sure.

FALDER. I believe that, Mr. Cokeson. Nobody wishes you harm, but they down you all the same. This feeling—— [*He stares round him, as though at something closing in.*] It's crushing me. [*With sudden impersonality*] I know it is.

COKESON. [*Horribly disturbed*] There's nothing there! We must try and take it quiet. I'm sure I've often had you in my prayers. Now leave it to me. I'll use my gumption and take 'em when they're jolly.

[*As he speaks the two partners come in.*

COKESON. [*Rather disconcerted, but trying to put them all at ease*] I didn't expect you quite so soon. I've just been having a talk with this young man. I think you'll remember him.

JAMES. [*With a grave, keen look*] Quite well. How are you, Falder?

WALTER. [*Holding out his hand almost timidly*] Very glad to see you again, Falder.

FALDER. [*Who has recovered his self-control, takes the hand*] Thank you, sir.

COKESON. Just a word, Mr. James. [*To* FALDER, *pointing to the clerks' office*] You might go in there a minute. You know your way. Our junior won't be coming this morning. His wife's just had a little family.

[FALDER *goes uncertainly out into the clerks' office.*

COKESON. [*Confidentially*] I'm bound to tell you all about it. He's quite penitent. But there's a prejudice against him. And you're not seeing him to advantage this morning; he's undernourished. It's very trying to go without your dinner.

JAMES. Is that so, Cokeson?

COKESON. I wanted to ask you. He's had his lesson. Now *we* know all about him, and we want a clerk. There is a young fellow applying, but I'm keeping him in the air.

JAMES. A gaol-bird in the office, Cokeson? I don't see it.

WALTER. "The rolling of the chariot-wheels of Justice!" I've never got that out of my head.

JAMES. I've nothing to reproach myself with in this affair. What's he been doing since he came out?

COKESON. He's had one or two places, but he hasn't kept them. He's sensitive—quite natural. Seems to fancy everybody's down on him.

JAMES. Bad sign. Don't like the fellow—never did from the first. "Weak character" 's written all over him.

WALTER. I think we owe him a leg up.

JAMES. He brought it all on himself.

WALTER. The doctrine of full responsibility doesn't quite hold in these days.

JAMES. [*Rather grimly*] You'll find it safer to hold it for all that, my boy.

WALTER. For oneself, yes—not for other people, thanks.

JAMES. Well! I don't want to be hard.

COKESON. I'm glad to hear you say that. He seems to see something [*spreading his arms*] round him. 'Tisn't healthy.

JAMES. What about that woman he was mixed up with? I saw someone uncommonly like her outside as we came in.

COKESON. *That!* Well, I can't keep anything from you. He has met her.

JAMES. Is she with her husband?

COKESON. No.

JAMES. Falder living with her, I suppose?

COKESON. [*Desperately trying to retain the new-found jollity*] I don't know that of my own knowledge. 'Tisn't my business.

JAMES. It's *our* business, if we're going to engage him, Cokeson.

COKESON. [*Reluctantly*] I ought to tell you, perhaps. I've had the party here this morning.

JAMES. I thought so. [*To* WALTER] No, my dear boy, it won't do. Too shady altogether!

COKESON. The two things together make it very awkward for you—I see that.

WALTER. [*Tentatively*] I don't quite know what we have to do with his private life.

JAMES. No, no! He must make a clean sheet of it, or he can't come here

WALTER. Poor devil!

COKESON. Will you have him in? [*And as* JAMES *nods*] I think I can get him to see reason.

JAMES. [*Grimly*] You can leave that to me, Cokeson.

WALTER. [*To* JAMES, *in a low voice, while* COKESON *is summoning* FALDER] His whole future may depend on what we do, dad.

[FALDER *comes in. He has pulled himself together, and presents a steady front.*

JAMES. Now look here, Falder. My son and I want to give you another chance; but there are two things I must say to you. In the first place: It's no good coming here as a victim. If you've any notion that you've been unjustly treated—get rid of it. You can't play fast and loose with morality and hope to go scot-free. If society didn't take care of itself, nobody would —the sooner you realize that the better.

FALDER. Yes, sir; but—may I say something?

JAMES. Well?

FALDER. I had a lot of time to think it over in prison. [*He stops.*

COKESON. [*Encouraging him*] I'm sure you did.

FALDER. There were all sorts there. And what I mean, sir, is, that if we'd been treated differently the first time, and put under somebody that could look after us a bit, and not put in prison, not a quarter of us would ever have got there.

JAMES. [*Shaking his head*] I'm afraid I've very grave doubts of that, Falder.

FALDER. [*With a gleam of malice*] Yes, sir, so I found.

JAMES. My good fellow, don't forget that you began it.

FALDER. I never wanted to do wrong.

JAMES. Perhaps not. But you did.

FALDER. [*With all the bitterness of his past suffering*] It's knocked me out of time. [*Pulling himself up.*] That is, I mean, I'm not what I was.

JAMES. This isn't encouraging for us, Falder.

COKESON. He's putting it awkwardly, Mr. James.

FALDER. [*Throwing over his caution from the intensity of his feeling*] I mean it, Mr. Cokeson.

JAMES. Now, lay aside all those thoughts, Falder, and look to the future.

FALDER. [*Almost eagerly*] Yes, sir, but you don't understand what prison is. It's here it gets you. [*He grips his chest.*

COKESON. [*In a whisper to* JAMES] I told you he wanted nourishment.

WALTER. Yes, but, my dear fellow, that'll pass away. Time's merciful.

FALDER. [*With his face twitching*] I hope so, sir.

JAMES. [*Much more gently*] Now, my boy, what you've got to do is to put all the past behind you and build yourself up a steady reputation. And that brings me to the second thing. This woman you were mixed up with—you must give us your word, you know, to have done with that. There's no chance of your keeping straight if you're going to begin your future with such a relationship.

FALDER. [*Looking from one to the other with a hunted expression*] But, sir . . . but, sir . . . it's the one thing I looked forward to all that time. And she too . . . I couldn't find her before last night.

[*During this and what follows* COKESON *becomes more and more uneasy.*

JAMES. This is painful, Falder. But you must see for yourself that it's impossible for a firm like this to close its eyes to everything. Give us this proof of your resolve to keep straight, and you can come back—not otherwise.

FALDER. [*After staring at* JAMES, *suddenly stiffens himself*] I couldn't give her up. I couldn't! Oh, sir! I'm all she's got to look to. And I'm sure she's all I've got.

JAMES. I'm very sorry, Falder, but I must be firm. It's for the benefit of you both in the long run. No good can come of this connection. It was the cause of all your disaster.

FALDER. But, sir, it means—having gone through all that—getting broken up—my nerves are in an awful state—for nothing. I did it for her.

JAMES. Come! If she's anything of a woman she'll see it for herself. She won't want to drag you down further. If there

10

were a prospect of your being able to marry her—it might be another thing.

FALDER.   It's not my fault, sir, that she couldn't get rid of him—she would have if she could.   That's been the whole trouble from the beginning.   [*Looking suddenly at* WALTER.] . . . If anybody would help her!   It's only money wanted now, I'm sure.

COKESON.   [*Breaking in, as* WALTER *hesitates, and is about to speak*]   I don't think we need consider that—it's rather far-fetched.

FALDER.   [*To* WALTER, *appealing*] He must have given her full cause since; she could prove that he drove her to leave him.

WALTER.   I'm inclined to do what you say, Falder, if it can be managed.

FALDER.   Oh, sir!   [*He goes to the window and looks down into the street.*

COKESON.   [*Hurriedly*] You don't take me, Mr. Walter.   I have my reasons.

FALDER.   [*From the window*] She's down there, sir.   Will you see her?   I can beckon to her from here.

[WALTER *hesitates, and looks from* COKESON *to* JAMES.

JAMES.   [*With a sharp nod*] Yes, let her come.

[FALDER *beckons from the window.*

COKESON.   [*In a low fluster to* JAMES *and* WALTER] No, Mr. James.   She's not been quite what she ought to ha' been, while this young man's been away.   She's lost her chance.   We can't consult how to swindle the Law.

[FALDER *has come from the window.   The three men look at him in a sort of awed silence.*

FALDER.   [*With instinctive apprehension of some change—looking from one to the other*] There's been nothing between us, sir, to prevent it. . . . What I said at the trial was true.   And last night we only just sat in the Park.

[SWEEDLE *comes in from the outer office.*

COKESON.   What is it?

SWEEDLE.   Mrs. Honeywill.   [*There is silence.*

JAMES. Show her in.

[RUTH *comes slowly in, and stands stoically with* FALDER *on one side and the three men on the other. No one speaks.* COKESON *turns to his table, bending over his papers as though the burden of the situation were forcing him back into his accustomed groove.*

JAMES. [*Sharply*] Shut the door there. [SWEEDLE *shuts the door.*] We've asked you to come up because there are certain facts to be faced in this matter. I understand you have only just met Falder again.

RUTH. Yes—only yesterday.

JAMES. He's told us about himself, and we're very sorry for him. I've promised to take him back here if he'll make a fresh start. [*Looking steadily at* RUTH.] This is a matter that requires courage, ma'am.

[RUTH, *who is looking at* FALDER, *begins to twist her hands in front of her as though prescient of disaster.*

FALDER. Mr. Walter How is good enough to say that he'll help us to get a divorce.

[RUTH *flashes a startled glance at* JAMES *and* WALTER.

JAMES. I don't think that's practicable, Falder.

FALDER. But, sir——!

JAMES. [*Steadily*] Now, Mrs. Honeywill. You're fond of him.

RUTH. Yes, sir; I love him. [*She looks miserably at* FALDER.

JAMES. Then you don't want to stand in his way, do you?

RUTH. [*In a faint voice*] I could take care of him.

JAMES. The best way you can take care of him will be to give him up.

FALDER. Nothing shall make me give you up. You can get a divorce. There's been nothing between us, has there?

RUTH. [*Mournfully shaking her head—without looking at him*] No.

FALDER. We'll keep apart till it's over, sir; if you'll only help us—we promise.

JAMES. [*To* RUTH] You see the thing plainly, don't you? You see what I mean?

RUTH.   [*Just above a whisper*] Yes.

COKESON.   [*To himself*] There's a dear woman.

JAMES.   The situation is impossible.

RUTH.   Must I, sir?

JAMES.   [*Forcing himself to look at her*] I put it to you, ma'am. His future is in your hands.

RUTH.   [*Miserably*] I want to do the best for him.

JAMES.   [*A little huskily*] That's right, that's right!

FALDER.   I don't understand.   You're not going to give me up—after all this?   There's something—— [*Starting forward to* JAMES.] Sir, I swear solemnly there's been nothing between us.

JAMES.   I believe you, Falder.   Come, my lad, be as plucky as she is.

FALDER.   Just now you were going to help us.   [*He stares at* RUTH, *who is standing absolutely still; his face and hands twitch and quiver as the truth dawns on him.*]   What is it?   You've not been——

WALTER.   Father!

JAMES.   [*Hurriedly*] There, there!   That'll do, that'll do! I'll give you your chance, Falder.   Don't let me know what you do with yourselves, that's all.

FALDER.   [*As if he has not heard*] Ruth?

[RUTH *looks at him; and* FALDER *covers his face with his hands.   There is silence.*

COKESON.   [*Suddenly*] There's someone out there.   [*To* RUTH.] Go in here.   You'll feel better by yourself for a minute.

[*He points to the clerks' room and moves towards the outer office.* FALDER *does not move.* RUTH *puts out her hand timidly.   He shrinks back from the touch.   She turns and goes miserably into the clerks' room.   With a brusque movement he follows, seizing her by the shoulder just inside the doorway.* COKESON *shuts the door*]

JAMES.   [*Pointing to the outer office*] Get rid of that, who ever it is.

SWEEDLE.   [*Opening the office door, in a scared voice*] Detective-Sergeant Wister.

[*The detective enters, and closes the door behind him.*

WISTER. Sorry to disturb you, sir. A clerk you had here, two years and a half ago. I arrested him in this room.

JAMES. What about him?

WISTER. I thought perhaps I might get his whereabouts from you. [*There is an awkward silence.*

COKESON. [*Pleasantly, coming to the rescue*] We're not responsible for his movements; you know that.

JAMES. What do you want with him?

WISTER. He's failed to report himself lately.

WALTER. Has he to keep in touch with the police then?

WISTER. We're bound to know his whereabouts. I dare say we shouldn't interfere, sir, but we've just heard there's a serious matter of obtaining employment with a forged reference. What with the two things together—we must have him.

[*Again there is silence.* WALTER *and* COKESON *steal glances at* JAMES, *who stands staring steadily at the detective.*

COKESON. [*Expansively*] We're very busy at the moment. If you could make it convenient to call again we might be able to tell you then.

JAMES. [*Decisively*] I'm a servant of the Law, but I dislike peaching. In fact, I can't do such a thing. If you want him you must find him without us.

[*As he speaks his eye falls on* FALDER'S *cap, still lying on the table, and his face contracts.*

WISTER. [*Noting the gesture—quietly*] Very good, sir. I ought to warn you that sheltering——

JAMES. I shelter no one. But you mustn't come here and ask questions which it's not my business to answer.

WISTER. [*Dryly*] I won't trouble you further then, gentlemen.

COKESON. I'm sorry we couldn't give you the information. You quite understand, don't you? Good-morning!

[WISTER *turns to go, but instead of going to the door of the outer office he goes to the door of the clerks' room.*

COKESON. The other door . . . the other door!

[WISTER *opens the clerks' door.* RUTH'S *voice is heard:* "Oh, do!" *and* FALDER'S: "I can't!" *There is a little pause; then,*

with sharp fright, RUTH *says:* "Who's that?" WISTER *has
gone in.*   [*The three men look aghast at the door.*

WISTER.   [*From within*] Keep back, please!

[*He comes swiftly out with his arm twisted in* FALDER'S.   *The
latter gives a white, staring look at the three men.*

WALTER.   Let him go this time, for God's sake!

WISTER.   I couldn't take the responsibility, sir.

FALDER.   [*With a queer, desperate laugh*] Good!

[*Flinging a look back at* RUTH, *he throws up his head, and goes
out through the outer office, half dragging* WISTER *after him.*

WALTER.   [*With despair*] That finishes him.   It'll go on for
ever now.

[SWEEDLE *can be seen staring through the outer door.   There
are sounds of footsteps descending the stone stairs; suddenly a dull
thud, a faint* "My God!" *in* WISTER'S *voice.*

JAMES.   What's that!

[SWEEDLE *dashes forward.   The door swings to behind him.
There is dead silence.*

WALTER.   [*Starting forward to the inner room*] The woman
—she's fainting!

[*He and* COKESON *support the fainting* RUTH *from the doorway
of the clerks' room.*

COKESON.   [*Distracted*] Here, my dear!   There, there!

WALTER.   Have you any brandy?

COKESON.   I've got sherry.

WALTER.   Get it, then.   Quick!

[*He places* RUTH *in a chair—which* JAMES *has dragged forward.*

COKESON.   [*With sherry*] Here!   It's good strong sherry.

                              [*They try to force the sherry between her lips.*
                              [*There is the sound of feet, and they stop to listen.*

[*The outer door is reopened—*WISTER *and* SWEEDLE *are seen
carrying some burden.*

JAMES.   [*Hurrying forward*] What is it?

[*They lay the burden down in the outer office, out of sight, and
all but* RUTH *cluster round it, speaking in hushed voices.*

WISTER.   He jumped—neck's broken.

WALTER. Good God!

WISTER. He must have been mad to think he could give me the slip like that. And what was it—just a few months!

WALTER. [*Bitterly*] Was that all?

JAMES. What a desperate thing! [*Then, in a voice unlike his own.*] Run for a doctor—you! [SWEEDLE *rushes from the outer office.*] An ambulance!

[WISTER *goes out. On* RUTH'S *face an expression of fear and horror has been seen growing, as if she dared not turn towards the voices. She now rises and steals towards them.*

WALTER. [*Turning suddenly*] Look!

[*The three men shrink back out of her way.* RUTH *drops on her knees by the body.*

RUTH. [*In a whisper*] What is it? He's not breathing. [*She crouches over him.*] My dear! My pretty!

[*In the outer office doorway the figures of men are seen standing.*

RUTH. [*Leaping to her feet*] No, no! No, no! He's dead!
[*The figures of the men shrink back.*

COKESON. [*Stealing forward. In a hoarse voice*] There, there, poor dear woman!

[*At the sound behind her* RUTH *faces round at him.*

COKESON. No one'll touch him now! Never again! He's safe with gentle Jesus!

[RUTH *stands as though turned to stone in the doorway staring at* COKESON, *who, bending humbly before her, holds out his hand as one would to a lost dog.*

The curtain falls.

JOHN GALSWORTHY

1867—1933

IN John Galsworthy's earlier years no one could possibly have
seen in him a world-famous author or indeed any kind of
writer at all. Yet he became one of the most outstanding
English novelists and dramatists of his time, and received the
highest national and international honours. Moreover there
was nothing vulgar in his remarkable success story, for he
remained all his life unself-seeking, modest and generous, a
humane influence in British and international affairs.

John Galsworthy (he pronounced it *Gollsworthy*) was born
at Kingston, near London, on August 14th, 1867, the son of a
wealthy London solicitor and property owner, the original of
Old Jolyon in *The Forsyte Saga*, whose ancestors were small
farmers in Devonshire. John was educated at Harrow, one of
the most famous and exclusive of English public schools,
where he was Captain of Football, and at New College,
Oxford, where he studied law. He went on to Lincoln's Inn,
one of the ancient legal societies in London which maintain
the standards of legal qualifications and conduct, and in 1890
he was called to the Bar, that is, he qualified as a barrister, who
could conduct cases in the higher courts of law. He had no
need to earn his living and he never practised law, but no
doubt the legal training strengthened his natural tendency to
judicious impartiality of mind and precision in the use of words.
It is equally significant that he was born and grew up in the
nineteenth century heyday of British prosperity, when the
progress of civilization seemed assured and such barbarous
catastrophes as the two world wars were unthinkable. John
Galsworthy, a well-to-do young man about town, complete
even to a monocle, seemed destined to remain shut up in that
self-satisfied, comfortable little world to which most of the
characters in his novels and plays belong.

An aimless social existence did not long appeal to him, however. He travelled adventurously in the Pacific and the Far East, and on the voyage home he met Joseph Conrad, the Polish seaman who became a great English novelist and Galsworthy's lifelong friend. He met other people who unsettled him. He began to discover the dreadful London slums of that time, from some of which his father drew rents, and he was horrified by what he found. The hypocrisy of his own class became intolerable to him. Most disturbing of all he fell deeply in love with his cousin's exceptionally beautiful and talented wife, Ada Galsworthy, who was very unhappy in her marriage. For ten years they maintained a secret love affair, often travelling abroad together. In those days a divorce was a major social sensation and Galsworthy's father would have been deeply distressed by it, so the lovers waited until after his death. They were married in 1905, and John Galsworthy remained devoted to Ada all his life. Some people thought him slavishly devoted.

Because she had been divorced she was shunned by most of their acquaintances, and it was this, coming when he was already deeply unsettled, which finally made Galsworthy rebel against the social class to which he belonged, while it was she who made him into a writer. Although there was no evidence at all except her own intuition, she was absolutely convinced of his latent ability, and reluctant as he was he could not refuse her anything. She helped and encouraged him constantly for the rest of his life. They discussed every detail of his work, and she typed nearly all of it herself, often three times over, for he revised everything meticulously. When he was writing with difficulty nothing helped him so much as her playing to him; she was a fine pianist and they both loved music.

His first book was a volume of feeble and imitative short stories, *From the Four Winds*, published in 1897. This was a failure in every way, and other failures followed, but the tide began to turn with his third novel *The Island Pharisees* (1904); and his fourth, *The Man of Property* (1906) was the first of his chronicles of the Forsyte family. Some people think it is his

best work. He published nineteen novels between 1900 and
1933, besides many short stories, but his fame rests mainly on
the numerous Forsyte novels and stories, which were collected
as *The Forsyte Saga* (1922), *A Modern Comedy* (1929) and *End
of the Chapter* (1935), and which achieved such an immense
success on television nearly forty years later. Fastidiously
written, like all his work, the early Forsyte novels show
Galsworthy's shrewd observation of the class against which he
had rebelled, the rich merchants who then governed Britain
and who were sometimes so possessed by their love of money
and property that as human beings they were destroyed by it.
But the later novels, in which he arraigned the young people of
the nineteen-twenties, sentimentalized the older Forsytes
into much less unsympathetic figures. In fact the youthful rebel
became the elderly conservative, as rebels so often do, but not
before his writings and personal influence had contributed
valuably to the movement towards greater social justice.

The novels show also his compassionate sympathy for the
poor and oppressed, although he never understood them as
well as he understood the rich. It is a powerful sympathy,
which shows most clearly in his plays, many of which, from
The Silver Box (1906) onwards, are clearly the work of a social
reformer. He wrote twenty full-length plays and a number
of short ones, and published also numerous volumes of verse,
essays and lectures.

As his fame and popularity grew he mellowed into the
eminent and widely respected man of letters. He and his wife
were well received everywhere. He refused a knighthood, but
accepted a distinguished British honour, the Order of Merit,
in 1929, and honorary doctorates from many universities. He
was awarded the Nobel Prize for Literature in 1932, and
characteristically he gave the prize money to the P.E.N., the
international fellowship of writers of which he was the first
President. It still flourishes, and its objects are still those so
dear to Galsworthy's heart: "to promote the friendly co-
operation of writers in every country in the interests of
literature, freedom of expression and international goodwill."

Apart from an interlude of hospital work, with his wife, during the First World War (and he loathed war), Galsworthy lived the quiet life of a successful man of letters who loved dogs and horses and worked hard. He usually gave away half his income, and he lived on a modest scale in London, Devonshire and elsewhere, but he and Ada travelled very widely about the world, mainly at her instigation. His large and continuous literary output and his travels would have been more than enough for most men, but all through his working life he gave much of his time to social and political causes, among them slum clearance, a minimum wage for workers in "sweated" industries, reforms in the divorce law and the prison system, votes for women, improvements in slaughter houses, and better working conditions for ponies in mines. The help which he gave privately to innumerable people in need was never publicized.

He died at Grove Lodge, Hampstead, in north London, on January 31st, 1933.

JUSTICE

IT is as the author of *Justice* that Galsworthy the social reformer is most often remembered, and rightly, for no other
work of his made such a powerful impact on the English
social conscience or produced such immediate results.

All the circumstances combined to this end. The Liberal
Government, which had come into power in 1905, was laying
the foundations of the present Welfare State by a great series
of social and political reforms, which included the first Old
Age Pensions, National Health Insurance and a limited
Unemployment Insurance. At the same time the Labour
Party was emerging as a new power, in the House of Commons
and in the country. There were still plenty of people ready to
attack Galsworthy's work as "dangerous and revolutionary,"
but the "climate of opinion" was already beginning to change
in his favour when his first play, *The Silver Box*, was written,
and was more favourable when *Justice*, his fourth play,
appeared in 1910. Moreover many special factors, to be
considered later, prepared the way for *Justice*, besides his
growing reputation as novelist and dramatist.

When *The Silver Box* was performed at the Court Theatre,
London, in 1906, soon after his thirty-ninth birthday, it
became at once the most discussed and controversial play of
that year. The Court Theatre was then making theatrical
history—just as, exactly fifty years later, it made history again
with John Osborne's *Look Back in Anger*. The series of new
plays produced at the Court Theatre from 1904 to 1907,
brilliantly directed by J. E. Vedrenne and Harley Granville-
Barker, was a major landmark in the history of English drama:
it included new plays by Shaw, Yeats, Granville-Barker,
Gilbert Murray, Masefield and Galsworthy, and it began the
modern era.

The Silver Box showed that a new dramatist had appeared, with a style and attitude of his own. His aim, as he said later himself, was "to create such an illusion of actual life passing on the stage as to compel the spectator to pass through an experience of his own, to think and talk and move with the people he sees thinking and talking and moving in front of him." Moreover Galsworthy gave the audience something important to think and talk about, a social problem or a question of conscience. *The Silver Box* was in fact a "play of ideas."

So many such plays have been written since that we take them for granted now, but in 1906 they were revolutionary, and often resented, for audiences of those days had long been accustomed to artificial plays written solely for light entertainment, with little truth to life and little artistic quality. The two great leaders in this theatrical revolution, which was European, were the Norwegian, Henrik Ibsen (1828–1906), whose plays were translated into English, and the Irishman, George Bernard Shaw (1856–1950). John Galsworthy followed with a less substantial but distinctively English contribution.

The new drama was by no means popular at first, but Galsworthy (with others) went on writing serious plays, and it was through these, rather than his novels, that he exercised his strongest influence for social reforms. Besides some shorter pieces, he wrote twenty full-length plays between 1906 and 1926, among the most notable being *The Silver Box* (1906), *Strife* (1909), *Justice* (1910), *Loyalties* (1922) and *Escape* (1926).

The theme of *The Silver Box* was that there was "one law for the rich and another for the poor." *Strife* dealt poignantly with a struggle between employers and workmen. *Justice* had a theme which was even nearer to Galsworthy's heart because he had been deeply conscious of it for so long. Living in a Devonshire farmhouse on the edge of Dartmoor, one of the wildest and loneliest districts in England, he was painfully aware of the grim convict prison in the middle of Dartmoor,

for there was nothing he hated more than the imprisonment
of living creatures, human or animal.*

In 1907 he visited the prison, and as a result he began a
public campaign for the abolition of the worst feature of
prison life, the period of solitary confinement (from three to
nine months) with which every convict began his punishment.
Galsworthy succeeded in arousing so much public feeling that
in September 1909 the initial period of solitary confinement
was reduced to three months for all prisoners.

Meanwhile he had been writing *Justice*, his second play
about crime and punishment, and his campaign had (quite
unintentionally) given it great advance publicity. When it
was performed in London on February 21st, 1910, the effect
—especially of the solitary confinement scene—was sensa-
tional. Even one of his least friendly critics, the novelist H. G.
Wells, wrote to him: "I've always opposed myself to your
very austere method hitherto. I've not liked a sort of cold
hardness in much of your work, but since it leads you at last
to the quite tremendous force of the play—well, I give in."

Galsworthy continued his campaign to get solitary confinement abolished altogether. He was soon conducting a controversial but very friendly correspondence with Mr. Winston
Churchill (later Sir Winston) who was then Home Secretary
and therefore responsible for prisons. In the end solitary
confinement was further reduced, to three months for persistent
criminals and one month for others, and Mr. Churchill
informed Galsworthy that *Justice* had played "a most important
part" in bringing this about. No other play in the five hundred
years of English drama has had a comparable effect.

In this campaign, as in everthing else, Galsworthy was
entirely sincere, but since he was always more artist than
reformer he became rather aggrieved that *Justice* was being
valued more highly as propaganda than as drama. A decade
later he wrote, perhaps rather inconsistently, in the collected
edition of his works: "A dramatist [he means himself]

---

* One of his later plays *Escape* (1926) is entirely concerned with a convict's attempt to escape
from Dartmoor prison.

strongly and pitifully impressed by the encircling pressure of modern environments . . . will not write plays detached from the movements and problems of his times. He is not conscious, however, of any desire to solve those problems in his plays or to effect great reforms. His only ambition in drama, as in his other work, is to present truth as he sees it and, gripping with it his readers or his audience, to produce in them a sort of mental and moral ferment, whereby vision may be enlarged, imagination livened and understanding promoted."

These are the aims of all great art. It is for the readers and the theatre audiences of today to decide whether Galsworthy attained them in *Justice*, whether its success was merely topical or whether it has the permanent value of dramatic literature, by which vision is enlarged.

HOW FAR HAVE WE UNDERSTOOD?

POINTS FOR DISCUSSION AND COMPOSITION

Act I

1. What does James How mean by, "Well, Cokeson! There's something in character, isn't there?"?

2. Why does Falder say "It *is* too late"?

3. When do you first begin to suspect Falder and why?

4. For the dramatist one of the most difficult parts of a play is the exposition; he has to introduce his characters to the audience, explain their relationship to each other and the situation in general, and give any information which may be necessary about previous events. The problem is to do all this without making it too obvious that it is being done, and at the same time to catch the interest of the audience. The worst method is that which Shakespeare, with unusual carelessness, used at the opening of *As You Like It*, when Orlando makes

a long, dull speech telling Adam many things which Adam must quite obviously know already. Do you think that Galsworthy has managed the exposition well?

5. "He has dissolute habits," says James How. "He's gone to work in the most cold-blooded way to defraud his employers and cast the blame on an innocent man." Do you agree?

6. Compare the attitudes of James How, Walter How and Cokeson to Falder in this scene. What differences in character do they show?

7. The characters in a play should behave as their feelings, ideas and circumstances make them behave; they should not say or do things merely to help forward the plot. Why does Ruth Honeywill come to the office? It it because Galsworthy could think of no other way of making Falder's position clear, or are there convincing reasons for her coming?

8. If you had been in James How's position would you have prosecuted Falder or not? Why?

9. Some playwrights make all their characters speak alike. Has Galsworthy made this mistake, or do his characters speak distinctively, in accordance with their personalities?

10. What defects can you find in the structure of Act I?

Act II

11. Why is forgery regarded as a very serious crime?

12. Why did Galsworthy open this scene in the middle of the trial instead of starting at the beginning?

13. Are Galsworthy's own views apparent in this scene? If so, what are they and how are they shown?

14. If you had been a member of the jury what verdict would you have wanted to give, and why?

15. State the arguments for and against sending Falder to prison.

16. Compare Cleaver and Frome.

17. A trial scene is usually successful on the stage. Why is this?

18. Compare this trial with the trial in Galsworthy's first

play, *The Silver Box;* or with any other trial scene in a play which you know.

19. Where does the climax of this scene occur, the point of highest tension?

20. Explain the full meaning of the following and comment:

    (a) You are ranging rather far, Mr. Frome.

    (b) "It's a matter of life and death."

    (c) And did he button it when you called his attention to it?

    (d) Like a fate hanging over him.

    (e) I remember thinking of Mr. Cokeson's face.

21. Is the Judge's summing up, in his speech to the Jury, perfectly fair?

22. Frome's request that Ruth Honeywill's name should not be published might have been made later. Why does Galsworthy place it just after the Jury have retired?

23. Frome describes Falder as "weak and highly nervous." What signs of this, if any, does Falder show during the trial?

24. Imagine that you were a member of the Jury and write a letter to a friend giving a short account of the trial.

Act III, Scene I

25. What is the purpose of this scene? What would the play lose if it were omitted?

26. Why is the Chaplain introduced? What does he contribute to the effect of the scene?

27. Galsworthy sometimes gives directions which appear to be intended for the reader rather than the actors or the audience. Are there any in this scene?

28. When Cokeson makes his first exit "the three officials do not look at each other, but their faces wear peculiar expressions." What are their feelings?

29. Why has Galsworthy set this scene on Christmas Eve?

Act III, Scene II

30. What do the Governor's interviews with Moaney,

Clifton and O'Cleary contribute to the play? What bearing
have they on Falder and on Scene III?

31. Galsworthy's stage directions include some instructions as to how the characters move and speak. Which of those
in this scene would be most difficult for the actors to follow?
Can you suggest how they should be followed? Do any of
them seem impossible? If so, why has Galsworthy given them?

32. Explain the full meaning of the following, and comment:
(a) Look alive over it!
(b) I don't want any tales.
(c) But it's the great conversation I'd be havin'.
(d) I'm quite right in my head sir.
(e) If I once get away from physical facts I don't know
where I am.

33. Describe the Governor's treatment of Falder in this
scene and say what you think of it.

34. Since Christmas is for the Christian the time of peace
on earth and good will towards men, and a festival of family
reunion, what do you think of the conversation about Christmas between the Governor and Wooder?

35. What is the Governor's state of mind at the end of
this scene?

ACT III, SCENE III

36. The stage direction says that there is a copy of *Lorna
Doone* on the table. Comment on this.

37. This scene has always been tremendously effective and
moving in the theatre. Can you explain why? Would it be
more or less powerful if Falder spoke?

38. What is the significance, in the play, of the banging
on the cell doors with which the scene ends?

ACT IV

39. "When a man's down never hit 'im . . . Give him a
hand up," says Cokeson. Does he always live up to this?

40. What does Walter How mean by, "The doctrine of
full responsibility doesn't quite hold in these days"? How
would he apply it to Falder?

41. Explain fully the meaning of the following, and comment:

    (a) They've forgot (*i.e.* forgotten) what human nature's like.

    (b) You've not got heart disease?

    (c) You'll find it safer to hold it for all that, my boy.

    (d) It's for the benefit of you both in the long run.

    (e) Father! (Walter How's exclamation)

    (f) You see the thing plainly, don't you?

    (g) Was that all?

42. When is James How most cruel to Falder?

43. Are there any points in this scene at which James How surprises you? It so, when and why?

44. Is Cokeson's last speech in keeping with his character?

GENERAL

45. The essence of drama is conflict. It may be conflict between the two individuals; or between an individual and a group of people; or between an individual and the community or social order to which he belongs; or in an individual's own mind and heart—a conflict between love and duty, for example. What conflicts can you find in *Justice*?

46. Unlike Shakespeare, Galsworthy was writing for a theatre in which every scene was given a realistic stage-setting, so he could not have a large number of short scenes in different places, because this would have been too troublesome and expensive and would have destroyed the continuity of the play. He was therefore compelled to concentrate the action in a few places. Has this caused any weakness in the structure?

47. A dramatist has to give some preliminary information in order to make a later happening more understandable or effective; e.g. the banging on the doors at the end of Act III, Scene III, would not be nearly so effective, and might puzzle

the audience, if there had been no references to it in the two preceding scenes. What other examples of this technique are there in the play?

48. Why is a play like this called naturalistic or realistic? How does it differ from poetic drama such as Shakespeare's?

49. Where does the climax of the play occur—the point of highest tension?

50. What humorous relief is there in *Justice*? Would the play have been strengthened if there had been more of it?

51. At one point Galsworthy considered ending the play at the end of Act III. Later on he considered ending with Falder's second arrest, instead of his suicide. How would the play have gained or lost if Galsworthy had adopted either of these endings?

52. Rewrite the last two pages of the play to make it end with the second arrest of Falder.

53. Can you suggest how the play might have been given a happy ending, which carried conviction, or is this impossible for these people in these circumstances?

54. Which characters have important decisions to make, and at which points do they make them?

55. Is this a crime play, a play about a forgery?

56. Why is the play called *Justice*?

57. What have you learned from the play about the English prison system as it was in 1910? What do you think of it?

58. *Justice* makes trenchant criticisms of the legal system and penal system of England in 1910. What are these criticisms and, so far as you can judge, what are Galsworthy's own views on the points which he raises?

59. "It was't nice," says Cokeson more than once. When does he say it and what does it tell you about him?

60. Which of the characters do you like most? Which do you dislike most? If you were acting in a production of the play which part would you most like to take? Give your reasons for all your answers.

61. "I'm thinking of his future," says Cokeson. Does anyone else think of Falder's future?

62. It is necessary for the community to be protected against crime and criminals. Does Galsworthy make sufficient allowance for this?

63. Should prisons be intended to punish or to reform the prisoners?

64. "The crime committed by Falder against Society is venial in comparison with the crime committed by Society against humanity. To handle a weakling, driven in a moment of stress to offend against the laws of Property, as if he were a tough criminal, hardened in sinning, is as unjust as it is stupid, and this Galsworthy reveals with so much aptness and truth that the effect of the play on an audience is overwhelming" —Hermon Ould: *John Galsworthy*, 1934, page 38. What is there to be said for and against this view?

65. Is the play more Ruth Honeywill's tragedy than Falder's?

66. The student who wishes to understand and appreciate *Justice* should certainly read others of Galsworthy's works— and particularly one or more of the plays which deal with crime and punishment: *The Silver Box* (1906), *The First and the Last* (1919), *Loyalties* (1922), and *Escape* (1926). *The First and the Last* and *Loyalties* end with the suicide of the man who has committed the crime. Compare *Justice* in detail with one or more of these plays. (See page 120).

67. In Galsworthy *dénouements* have "a double meaning, triumph and defeat" says one of his Asian critics. "Physically the characters are defeated but there is a sense of triumph in their souls in such works as *The Mob, Strife, A Bit of Love, A Family Man, Escape, The Roof, Justice* . . ." Do you agree in the case of *Justice*? (*Denouement*—French, untwisting— means the unravelling of the plot at the end of a play or novel, the outcome.)

68. Compare *Justice* in general terms with any great tragedy which you know. Do you consider *Justice* a great tragedy, likely to become one of the classics of English drama, or was its appeal merely topical and temporary?

ACTING NOTES

A PLAY is written to be performed, and the printed text, like a musical score, is simply the basis for a performance. When reading to himself the reader should hear and see everything, and the practised, imaginative reader can stage a good performance in his own mind; but drama is a communal art, and it is only as a combination of sound, movement and pictorial effect, presented to an audience, that a play can come fully to life.

Any group of people studying this play for their own purposes should attempt at least a half-performance, walking about book in hand, and rehearsing some if not all of the scenes by reading them several times and trying to make improvements every time. If the group wish to please an audience they should not choose this play for performance unless they can cast it fairly well, and in particular they must have actors who can give acceptable renderings of Falder, Cookson and Ruth Honeywill.

The group must also have a producer whose rulings they will accept and who will take charge of the production in much the same way as a conductor takes charge of an orchestra. The producer is responsible for the artistic harmony and unity of the play in all its details, and the success of the performance will depend largely on his knowledge, imagination, tact, enthusiasm, and willingness to learn.

When the play has been chosen, application for permission to perform it should be made *at once* to The Secretary, The Incorporated Society of Authors, 84 Drayton Gardens, London S.W.10, giving the name of the amateur company and the number, place and dates of the performances they wish to give.

The other business arrangements should also be started well in advance, booking the hall, finding printers for posters, tickets and programmes, getting lighting equipment, stage settings and so on. A detailed list of everything which has to be done should be made at a very early stage, and responsibilities should be allocated in writing.

Several auditions—trial readings—may be necessary before all the parts are finally cast, and before rehearsals can begin the producer must study the play very thoroughly, with his cast and stage in mind. He must see and hear clearly everything which happens. He should make himself a prompt-book, by breaking up two copies of the play and sticking the leaves on alternate pages of an exercise book. This gives him space for a stage-plan, or a series of stage-plans, for every scene, showing the position of furniture, doors, etc., and the entrances, movements, groupings, exits, etc., of the players, with notes on lighting, "noises off," etc. Since the play is the work of a very skilful and experienced playwright the author's stage-directions should be followed if they suit the stage to be used and the producer's interpretation of the play.

Every player should have a copy of the play for himself, so that he can study it as a whole, but he should not begin learning his part by heart until after the first rehearsals have been held and he has been shown his entrances, exits, and most important movements, so that he can associate these with words from the start. He must then learn his part, and cues, as quickly as possible. If the rehearsals are not held on the stage, a plan of the stage must be marked out on the floor of the rehearsal room; otherwise the change to the stage may confuse movements and groupings very badly.

Most plays, even when they are as realistic as Galsworthy's, can be performed successfully on a curtained stage, but it is difficult to imagine Act III, Scenes II and III, of *Justice* being really effective without realistic settings of the prison cells—and the success of the whole play is largely dependent on Scene III.

If the stage is deep enough a possible compromise with realism is to have the prison corridor and the cells built of wood or wood and canvas and permanently erected at the back of the stage, to be hidden by curtains for the rest of the play;

and to make Falder's cell a sectional wooden box, with a ceiling if possible, which can be erected quickly near the front of the stage and "struck" quickly when the scene is over. It is extremely important that everything which Falder does in this cell should be visible to everyone in the audience.

For the trial scene, important though it is, a curtained stage will do quite well. It is essential however that the Judge, seated in a high-backed chair with a desk in front of him, should be on a dais which raises him above everyone else; the clerk and the other court officials, seated just below him, should be raised a little. The Jury should be on one side, sideways or back to the audience, facing both the Judge and the two counsel, Mr. Cleaver and Mr. Frome, on the opposite side, so that the counsel can address the Judge and the Jury, and question the witnesses, but can be clearly seen by the audience. They too should be above stage level. They must not be hidden by the witness-box or the dock in which the prisoner sits, both of which should be on the same side of the stage as the barristers.

Lighting is always important, but *Justice* gives little scope for subtlety or variation, except in Act III, Scene III. Lighting must be bright enough for faces to be clearly seen from the back of the hall. Headlights and footlights must be adjusted to eliminate unwanted shadows. Lighting and scene-changing rehearsals are essential if mistakes, delays and noise are to be avoided.

Costumes of 1910 are needed, for *Justice* is set in a vanished England, in the historic past before the First World War. There should be at least an attempt to suggest the dress of that time. The Judge wears a flowing red gown and a formal legal wig. The clerk of the court and the counsel wear black gowns, white linen strips ("bands") under their chins instead of ties, and formal legal wigs.